AF269334

In the Pale Blue Grass

Elle Daviau

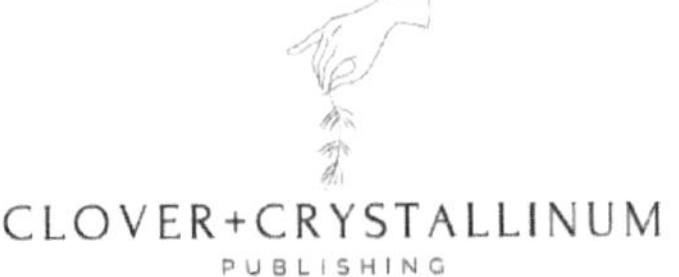

CLOVER+CRYSTALLINUM
PUBLISHING

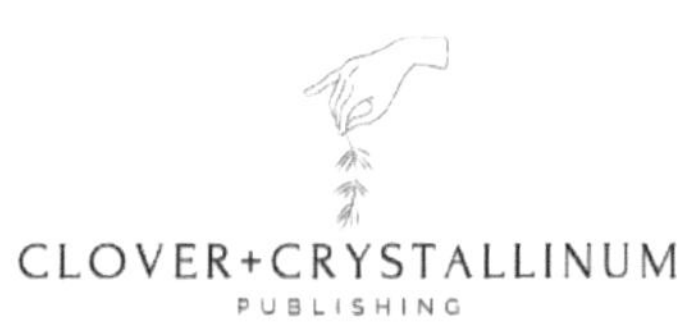

ISBN: 978-1-943337-83-5
pISBN: 978-1-943337-40-8
eISBN: 978-1-943337-41-5

Any references to historical events, real people, or real places are used fictitiously. Names, characters, and places are products of the author's imagination.

Published by: Clover + Crystallinum Publishing
Book Design - Cover & Interior
www.elledaviau.com/clover-crystallinum-publishing

Author website: http://www.elledaviau.com

Printed in the United States of America
Seattle, Washington

*Let your heart not ache
for those
who must be forgotten...*

Elle Daviau

In the Pale Blue Grass

Oh nature,
what have I done?
I lay quietly beneath
the trees that bend deeply
in the fabric of the sky.
Those trees that look black
in the absence of the sunlight.
They loom overhead and fill
my mind with woeful
sorrow and pathetic compulsion
for another look.
Another taste of your wicked desire.

Save me, Mother, from this torment
that my mind clamours for.
Save me from the longing of someone
just the same.

For yet another break,
I cannot bear.

Elle Daviau

In the Pale Blue Grass

Elle Daviau

Genesis 1:1

He unzipped her flowing dress, falling to the floor. She was an uncovered rare mystery— she was vulnerable.

What remained of her image was wrapped around her feet. He lifted her at her waist and picked her out of the fairy garden that she built around herself—such a place that dared to hide such beauty.

He holds the forbidden flower in his arms and lays her down on the sheet topped bed. Soft touches and gentle movements, he removes the last pieces of her mask, opening up the rest of her.

He moves down to her side. Here he did not move, not even breathe, for he did not know if what he was doing was okay.

His body told him otherwise, a single kiss upon her abdomen. Skin warming and fingers curling, they are at peace.

He finds himself in a dream-like state
where he drifts into oblivion with her at his side,
and they become one.

Elle Daviau

Elle Daviau

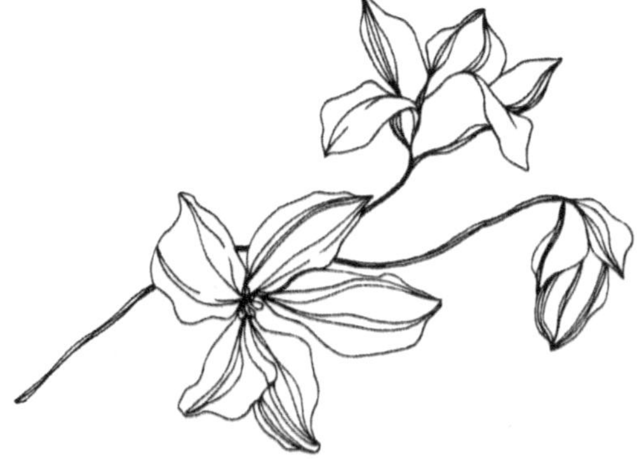

Narcissus - 凌遲

Angel lines, he held me in the moonlight.
The gliding through the night air
by soft feathers attached to strong wings.

I've lost my feathers.

Beware the one that wants your souvenir—
the one that wants to take a piece
of your incandescence
because they cannot create
this divinity themselves.

Plucking my feathers
and throwing them away
to cause my bloodshed—
death by a thousand cuts.

Blood flooding, staining these pretty white lines.
Dirtied skin, he left me nameless
and fallen in the daffodil fields.

I've forgotten who I am.

Elle Davia

Elle Daviau

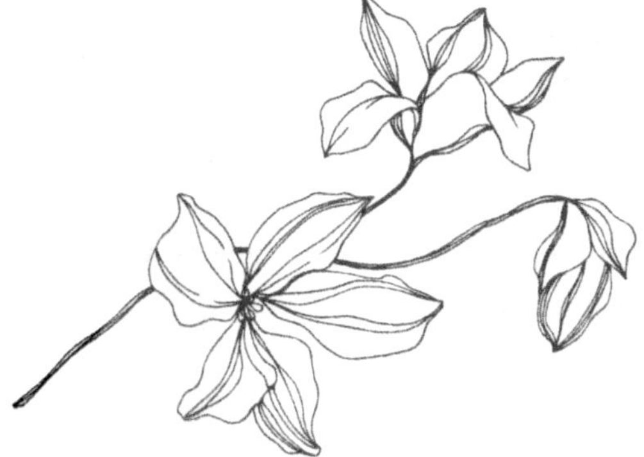

son of the dawn

I know the feeling:
the threatening desire
and necessary loss
for my basic needs,
just to be with you
because my infatuation tells me
you matter more than I.
These feelings forcing me to keep this tender
flame alive
even when it was always destined
to extinguish.

And instead of only killing this dark flame,
you obliterated me.

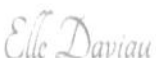

Elle Daviau

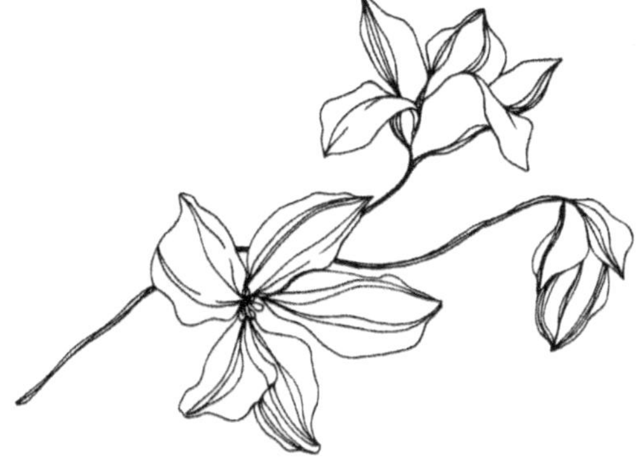

Days of Wine & Rose

Kiss me now, slow —

slowly, please.

Elle Daviau

s'énamourer

Three Minutes to midnight. 23:57
He's still next to me. Our soft bodies, ever so
still.
I feel his hands, his arms—they're rough
like he's seen the world, felt it through his skin
and still took the pain.

Two thirteen. 02:13
My eyes are frozen open
and pictures paint my mind. He's still wrapped
around my waist and I cannot let go.
My id clamours on,
        *You deserve nothing, no one. He's going to
see you soon—really see you.*
I wait for the thoughts to subside
and leave me in my false despair.

Three Thirty-two. 03:32
He's turned
on his back now and I'm free of his grasp.
I glance out the window, pale moonlight
shines down on his face,
evaporating all color.

The strong curves of his jaw, the arch of his
Grecian nose, they cast shadows—
he's become the dark side of the moon,
hiding the secrets
that I long to know.
Even now, peacefully asleep, his brows are
slightly furrowed.
His chest lifts deeply,
slowly.
With every breath I'm lost in this black and
white image of an angel.
A god?

Four seventeen. 04:17
I've forgotten
exactly what the color of his eyes look like
and I'm aching to know. Hands and chin rested
upon his chest, I wait.
I consider waking him.
I need to know. I need to remember
before he's taken from me.
Before
I let him go.

Before,
I push him away.

Four forty-seven. 04:47
Pale blue eyes flutter awake
and my heart gives in for a moment.
He sees me
and he smiles gently.
Those eyes,
a clear picture now — they're an angry ocean,
whitecaps intertwining
like spiderwebs over a dark horizon.
He takes my face in his hands
and kisses my lips.
He says softly against my cheek, *"I see you."*
His words whisper into the night,
in my half-dazed state,
washing a spell over me
and I drift into an ethereal sleep,
away from this waking dream.

Elle Daviau

Moonlight Felicity

Keep my dear children safe, will you?
Don't let them feel too much of the pain I felt, when
my heart broke,
>   the Moon said.

>   *Of course, my love,*
>   said the Sun.

>   Elle Daviau

Elle Daviau

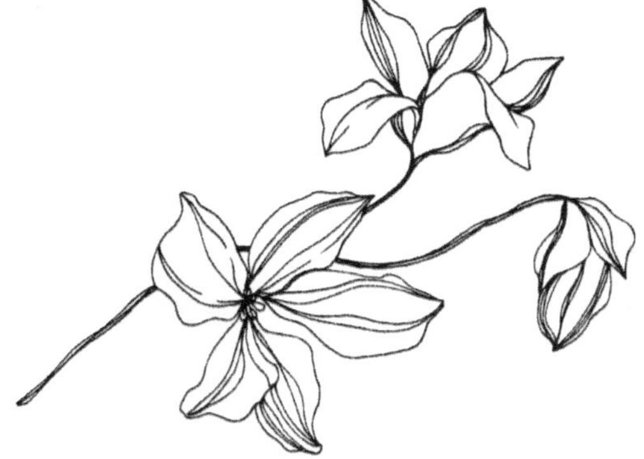

the moon garden —bloom &
desiccation

I go through phases of beauty and ugliness,
like a flower, going through cycles of bloom,
then those of growth. I cannot help when they
are, I can only prepare.

It's taken me many years to know this
and I cannot expect you to devote your life
to someone ever so changing,
someone so erratic, and exhausting
like me.

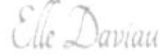

Elle Daviau

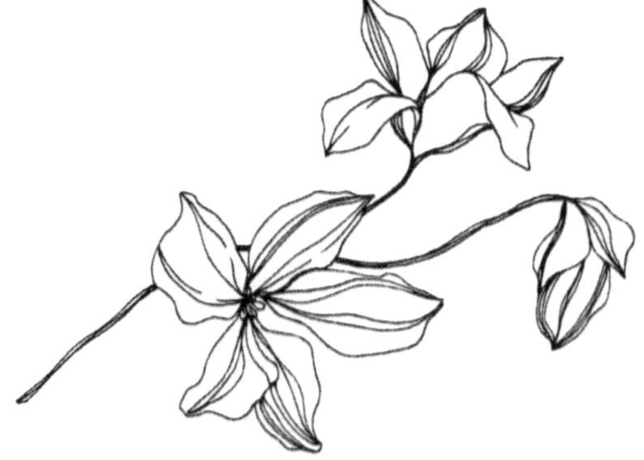

Wild Orchids

He laid me down
below the magnolia tree,

walked away
and left the little garden
to care for me.

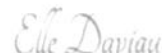

Elle Daviau

Elle Daviau

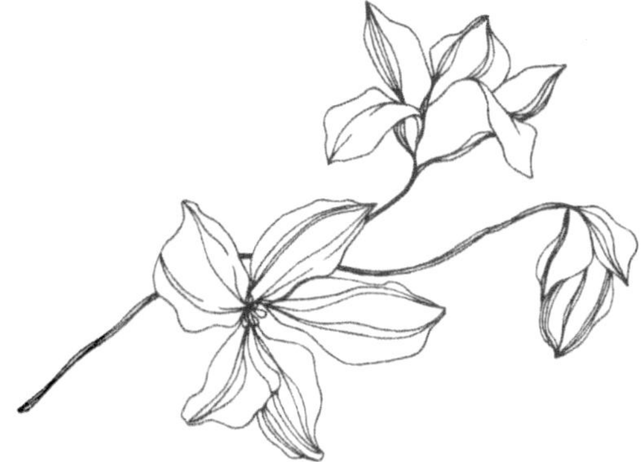

Wren of Lark

I'm met with one final kiss
it falls upon my lips
a kiss so still,
I can feel his heart beat into me.

Elle Daviau

Elle Daviau

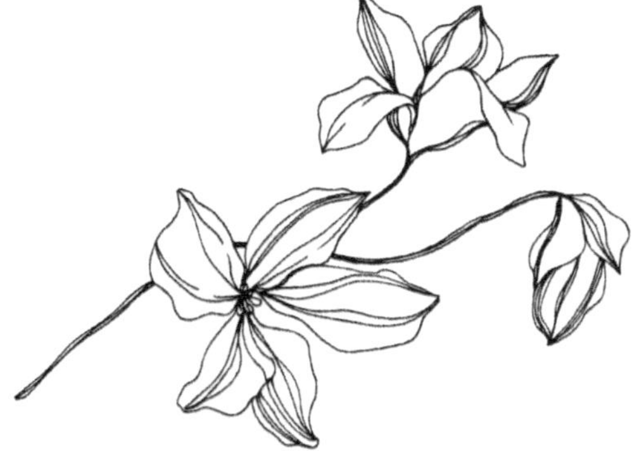

found in the lonely moments

When you love someone,
you see their soul

you feel who they are
it doesn't matter how long it's been
you know them
and their purpose
and you love them for it.

Elle Daviau

Elle Daviau

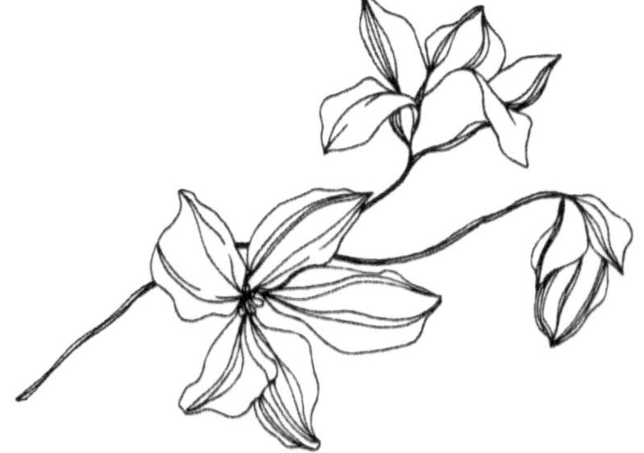

The Age of Aquarius

we bathe in the remains
of a fading hot pink sky
on late summer nights.

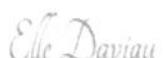

Elle Daviau

In the Pale Blue Grass

Elle Daviau

In the Pale Blue Grass

In the Pale Blue Grass

In the Pale Blue Grass

In the Pale Blue Grass

Elle Daviau

In the Pale Blue Grass

Elle Daviau

In the Pale Blue Grass

Sky Violette

I look away
from the person I know,

> Only to find
> when I look back
> I'm staring into the eyes of a stranger
> dressed in the skin
> of someone I thought I loved.

A stranger
with a low tolerance
for my insolence—
you won't deal with my bad behavior.

> At least
> not long enough
> for me to get away.

Elie Daviau

Elle Daviau

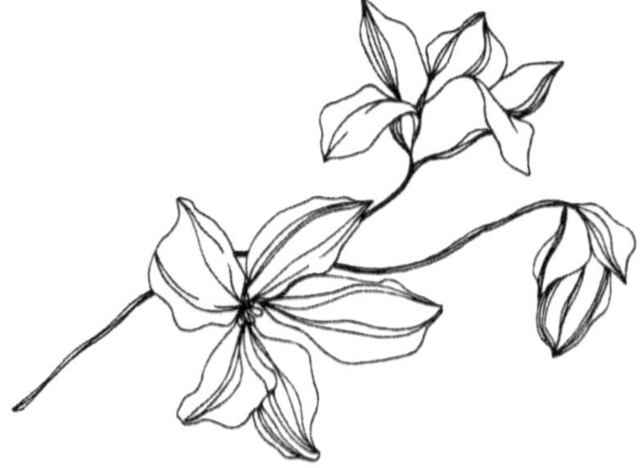

Amnesia

Forgetting - PART 1

I'm back
at the base
of the Japanese Maple Tree.
A light gaze
& A soft touch,
my chin on his chest.

I'm at ease.

Bruises
speak words,
painting my neck.
Trust,
they tell me,
trust, his lonely heart, in need of repair.

At ease, I feel.

Kisses,
they hurt,
like fine sugar crystals

surround his lips.
His sleepy eyes flutter
awake.

I feel longing.

A strawberry-colored moth
settles
on my skyward-facing hip,
It turns
to frail snow.

I need the taste.

A Calypso orchid
withers into the grass,
just as I.
Stone walls
lined with flowering vines
hold back my apathy.

Orange blossom flavors my mind.

My poor star that shines,
fading like the moon.

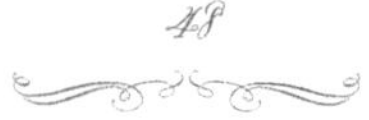

In the Pale Blue Grass

I'm reviving.

Tears shimmer
down my face.
I cannot see.
Sweet blushes

now become burning
slashes.

I wake from my dream.

At night,
Crescent City
waits for me.
I'll leave soon,
I told myself
last year.

He holds me down.

Touches my face,
luring me
back into my nightmare.

Elle Daviau

Impressionism
Forgetting - PART 2

I am wondering how I should continue. I have
the bones of the concept down,
but do I manipulate the reality of the picture to
make it more artful
or do I keep it realistic?

I'm wondering if impressionism is like our
memories—where copies of copies become
warped reflections looking back at me.

The details soon tainted and the colors
changed—the realities different.

Everything altered, but still the same shadow of
a reflection in the back of your mind.

Reminding: remembering a phantom of a
thought,
or maybe it was real.

Impressionism, is that not you?

In the Pale Blue Grass

Might I be wrong in my thinking that
impressionism is actually real
because a memory and a former thought is only
as good as its holder
because memories fade,
and they form into new creations.

Can our minds not manipulate themselves
into what they want us to see?

Is that not how a mind heals from a trauma?
I'd like to think
my mind protects me.
I cannot remember
what it felt like to be emotionally hurt, but I
know that it did.
I know it did—so it's real.

I'm not mistaken by that,
but people believe in religion—how can they
know if God is real?
They cannot, but they ever so believe.
So, to believe in something so strongly makes it
real, too.
If so, then is what I believe my past to be, also
real?

What my mind manipulated,
to save me from trauma, into something new,
a happy memory—that's real.

I believe my mind.
I trust my mind,
but I cannot help but question
its judgment.

Is it trauma
that I'm being saved from,
or my own thoughts?
If I could remember the feeling
of being hurt would I want to stay away
from being hurt again?
Is my mind telling me to stay away
from trauma now?

Could my mind's efforts
to protect me be working too well?
It's true,
I cannot remember,
but why do I get the urge
to feel it again.

Impressionism is a work of art
dictating my thoughts,

In the Pale Blue Grass

my memories,
dictating my actions now.

If I allow it to happen
am I contributing to my mind's own
destruction?
No.
Wallflowers climb these enormous walls
that hold in my bad memories.

They're a favor that my mind is letting me keep.
Allowing me to continue to see beauty in the
new without being ruined by the old.

Impressionism.
It's making me think
realism is not so real
as it is made out to be.

Impressionism is my mind,
and my mind is real—and that, I trust.
My mind is telling me remember,
but impressionism
is what I feel.

Elle Daviau

Elle Daviau

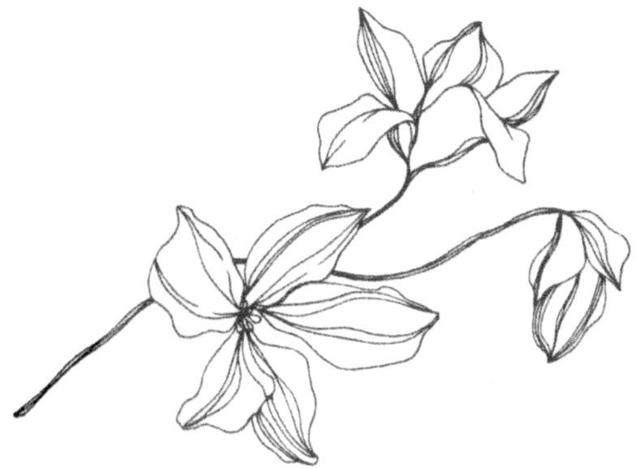

Vétheuil Gardens

Sunlight sparkles
in the droplets left
on the deciduous leaves.

Moving with the wind,
together in its flow.

Reminding me I cannot endure
much longer.

Elie Daviau

white camaro, scarred knees

Leather seats in your Camaro warm my legs—
you come alive.
Touches creep through my skin,
come on, baby.

Constricting wrists fossilize cuts.
Kisses tangle me chaotic.
Smoke spills from your mouth,
get out.

Dust gathers.
You push me and I collide with the ground.
The moon is half-awake tonight.
Start crawling.

Dirt clots scrapes.
Liquor overflows behind your python eyes,
but dark desires can't heal my pure heart's pain.
Get up. Don't talk.

Twenty-three paces forward.
Decrepit trees bow below me,
the rocky cliff sweeps whispers around my head

In the Pale Blue Grass

Do it. For me. Please.

Wet socks, cherry red.
I turn to face you.
Icy wind bites my neck—I shiver.
Keep going.

Lip gloss washes over shimmering lips.
I can't hear you.
The water tears at the aching shore
& ocean spray keeps me awake.
When the next wave comes.

Footsteps: hollow taps atop stone.
Your shadowy reflection stares back at me in the
churning depths.
Rigid fingers drive into my spine.
Now.

Falling fuels regret.
The ocean swallows lost souls at night,
where drowning feels peaceful beneath the stars.

Elle Daviau

Elle Daviau

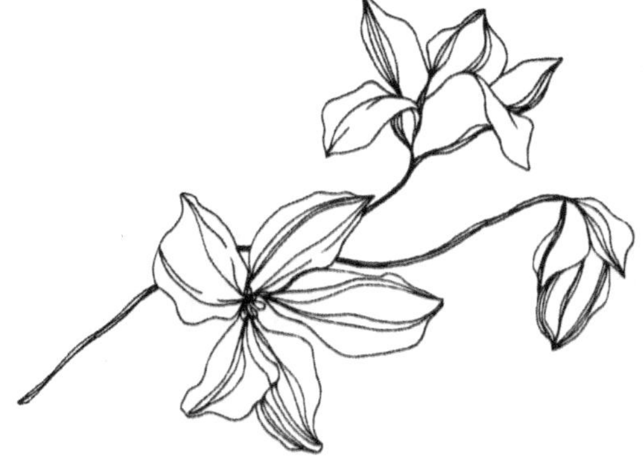

Actinomyces

Desiccation:

Earth worms floated to the surface of the grass
to escape drowning after every rainfall—
struggle to live, Mother Nature insisted,
she had only dealt them a bad hand.
I killed one after they poisoned me.

My petals will soon wilt,
my life will be drawn,
and the memory of my existence
soon just a dried flower cluttering the ground.

Elle Daviau

Serpentes

On **my** knees
I **feel** faint.
What, pray tell,
did you want from me?
                  I didn't like it any.

I **become** what you ask,
but I cannot maintain.
                  You didn't tell me much.

Save me from this holy fire.
Bite my lip and trust my impassivity.

Tell me.
Is this what you crave?
Keep me so very complete.
But I'm not.
I'm not complete at all.
I lack feeling.

You tell me, *oh, trust me, my sweet baby deer.*

I lack composure.

In the Pale Blue Grass

Trust me and I'll keep you safe.

I lack belonging.

Trust my words. Let them slip into the fractures that
worry has left in you.
Trust me. You can release my pain.

I need comfort
and I let you breathe.
You sink your venom in through my skin
and share your heart's heavy ache.

You slither away
and I'm free again.

But how can I be free?
I'm trapped
in your torment.

It's all yours
and you left with me.

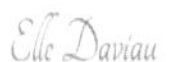

Elle Daviau

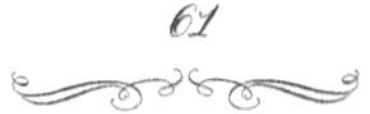

Elle Daviau

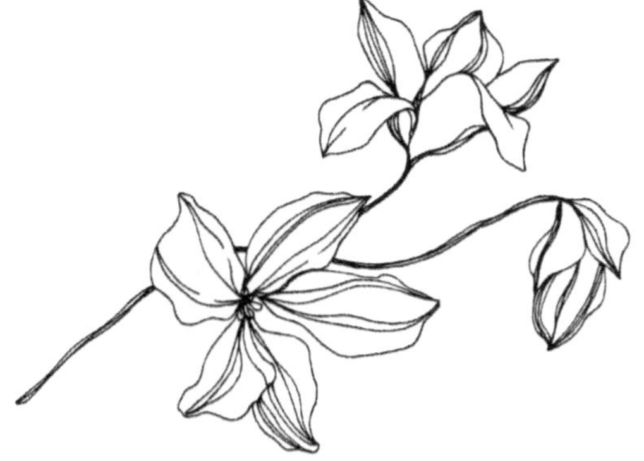

the dream

Asphyxiation was
    Trance-like kisses &
    faded bliss,

                sapping my body
              into delusional

death.

    Weakened, my fragile bones
      broke at the slightest touch

      the very same touch,
    that also put me to rest.

Elle Daviau

red and black veins

The North Star takes its time tonight,
and peaks through the dense clouds
only when safe.
It shines like my cherry lips.

Cryptic notes of mystery
sweep in on the tail feathers of a vicious wind
reminding me of the souls that rest easy here.
It smells like autumn.

I imagine sailboats marooned on beaches,
far from where I lay now, drenched
in the wet grass.
It comforts me.

New summer leaves disconnect reluctantly
and melt in the scattered rainfall.
My pale face mirrors the sky.
It fades like the moon tonight.

In the Pale Blue Grass

A cyclic mother tree imparts me;
for I am not wise,
I have little years on this earth.
It releases my trepidation.

I feel the need to decompose,
fester in the roots of the ground,
whisper to death, I need a second chance.
Then I can re-bloom where the rain precipitates
on the blades of the tall grass.

Elle Daviau

a posy of dragon snaps

he lived in her skin

a sickness that carried

glass shards through her veins.

He was the villain of her fable—

an undoing,

with a promised end.

And the unrest

that he had bore down

finally gave in.

In the Pale Blue Grass

In the legend of the flora, fauna, the creation of
the strawberry moon,
  and the girl with golden hair,

  she became an angel
    slain by the devil.

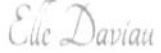

Elle Daviau

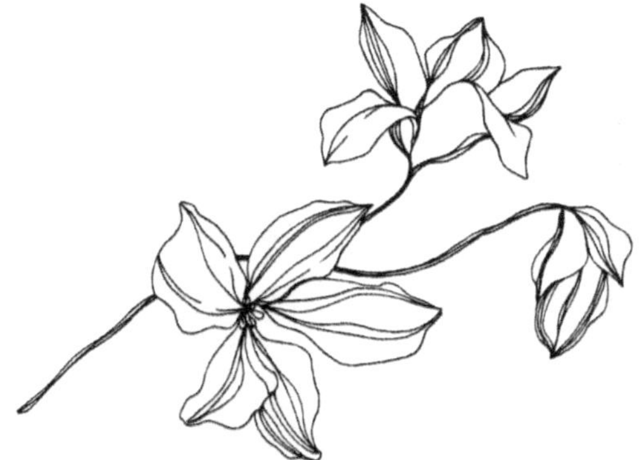

Apricity

How full sun and partial shade
have a completely different feeling
falling upon my skin.

The trees become sorrowful
when the sun disappears
behind dense cloud cover,
the end far from where we are now.

The end of your impertinence
in your touches for me,
and the beginning
of my convalescence.

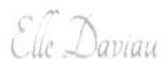

Elle Daviau

le sensation de noyade
Avec lui - PART 2

A sugar castle, far out in the beautiful
countryside.
You hold me captive.
Do I choose to stay?
Or am I forced?
A swamp surrounds me
and this moat keeps me
from my long-awaited distress.

Like phosphine
your scent infiltrated my lungs
with insanity and pungency,
but you no longer affect me.
I've grown immune,
becoming stronger and building my armour.

Moonlight that shines
through the bones of nature.
It illuminates the woodland creatures that hide
below in overgrown grass.
They're afraid of you, too.
They know to run away,
to veer from your grasp.

In the Pale Blue Grass

I'm hiding,
but your touch blooms flowers up my thighs
and lights fire beneath my abdomen.
My body tells me differently than my instincts.
This non-concordance creates confusion.

Or was this doubt yours?
Swimming becomes harder
with my arms tied behind my back.
Swimming: am I even real?
I feel as though if I let go I would just float.
My trepidation keeps me in place.

La mer—elle brille.
Bruises sparkle like ripened plums
with water shattered over their skin.
They look nice under the night sky.
I dread the sunrise bringing me back to my
desolation, where the beauty is washed away in
her celestial light.

Your voice echoes a waltz around my head—
I'm dizzy.

Drowsy daisies quickly crush beneath my feet,
but I cannot stop to care for the injuries

to their fragile stems and petals.
Your warm air rushes past my cheeks, every
second,
reliable as my racing heartbeat.

The candied apples
I long for when July comes
and this winter air
now feels like a warm summer breeze—
I've given in.

chills kiss my nose,
        my cheeks,
        my ears
      my feet crumble.
Where am I,
if I'm away from you?

Elle Daviau

Alexei

Part 1

to kiss,
to feel you.
I love skin that gleams like the summer moon.

Elle Daviau

Elle Daviau

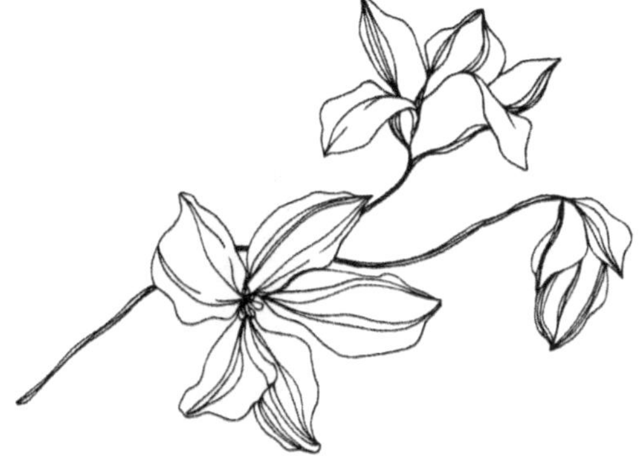

Nadezhda
Part 2

Strawberry vanilla curls cascade
down my back.

His rough hands collide
with my waist.

I find myself wishing for more.

To kiss
your blush-colored lips

and touch
such heavenly skin.

Elle Daviau

Elle Daviau

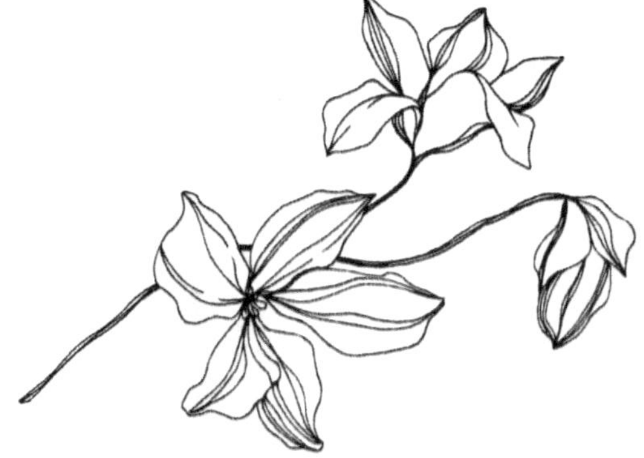

crystal child

how do you do it?

do what?

disconnect like that. from everyone.
so easily.

you have to make a clean cut. no going back.

and are you not lonely?

loneliness is worth not having to feel the pain.

Elle Daviau

Elle Daviau

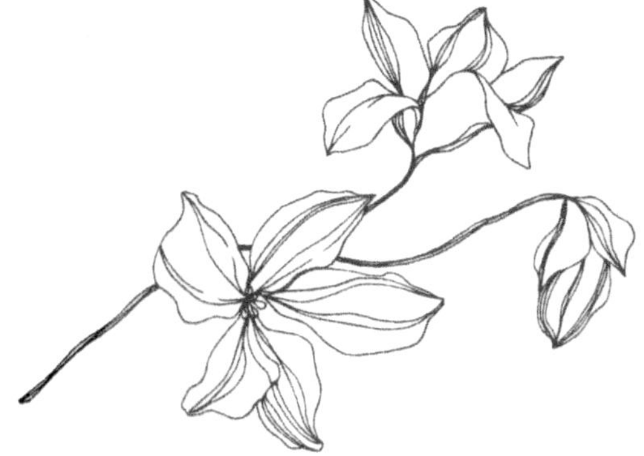

meadow mice

I lay upon your chest,
heavenly touches caress my face,

but I'm holding a ghost,
please don't let yourself fall away from this
body.

If you need to rest for a short time
I'll be here to care for you.

And when you're ready,
you'll wake in the meadows upon a bed of
wildflowers.

Elle Daviau

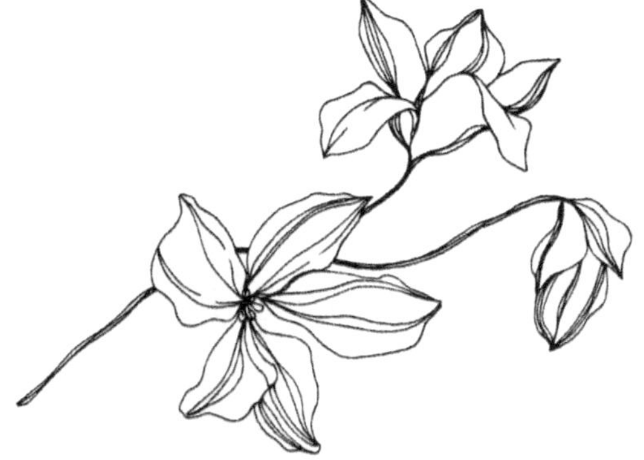

his words, a corduroy jacket & the stars in the sky

She took my hand as we were perched

atop a rocky ravine,

overlooking a plethora of forest.

Her tender skin,

warm beneath my rough palm,

How do you know it's going to be okay?

She smiles, and looks skyward.

Deep blue with crystal flecks swim

in her eyes.

A cool breeze crashes

over the slope of the cliff,

it takes the leaves and moves through her,

Because all of this beauty is made of the stars, as are

we.

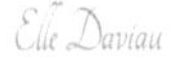
Elle Daviau

Elle Daviau

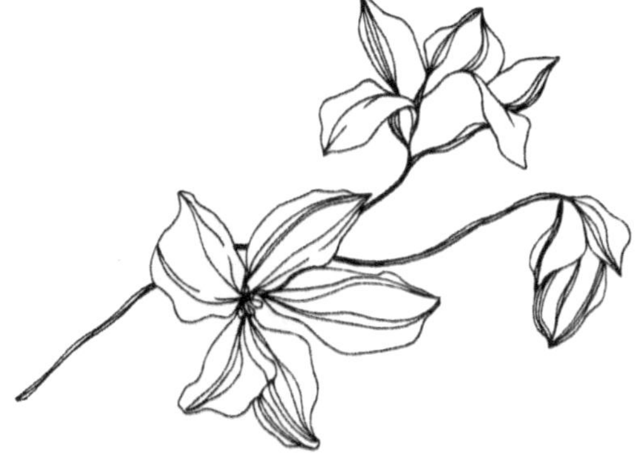

blue stormy skies

The midnight sun wrought with angels
swaying on their garlands of lore.
I soon drift from my stature,
down and across,
captured by this pain.

I rest below the ghastly oak,
with crawling roots
I am awfully coaxed.

Your arms lock—
they close me in
just as before.
This battle,
I'm ready to begin.

Elle Daviau

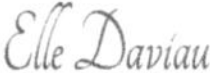

silver moon & glass is me

liquid silver, the moon dripped
upon the horizon.
These lovely sacred waters
filled with solemn souls touched—
reached for the one below my chest.
I cannot, I utter, *let this soul rest.*
She is young, her heart cannot be vain.

Wretched stars blink past dreary nights
against the pale black sky—forgotten they seem.
Sorely sour
with lost attention,
once so regent and perched atop velvet blue.

Deafening convoys sound of bout
they shadow my great sensibility.
Here I lay, at rest along the receding shore.
Tides bring me to where I must go. Abash my doubts
and offer me consolation.

But the waters are quiet, confirming what I
feared.

In the Pale Blue Grass

Crestfallen, movement unbearable,
limbs at rest,
but footsteps begin.

Soon—carefully I walk,
then stumble as a whisper begins.
I sit—I crumble and look up
with sorrow eyes
for it is the sky that speaks now.
Shining—whisking breathless words past and
through me
lighting the green in my eyes.
These words: *let your heart not ache for those who
must be forgotten.*

Elle Daviau

Elle Daviau

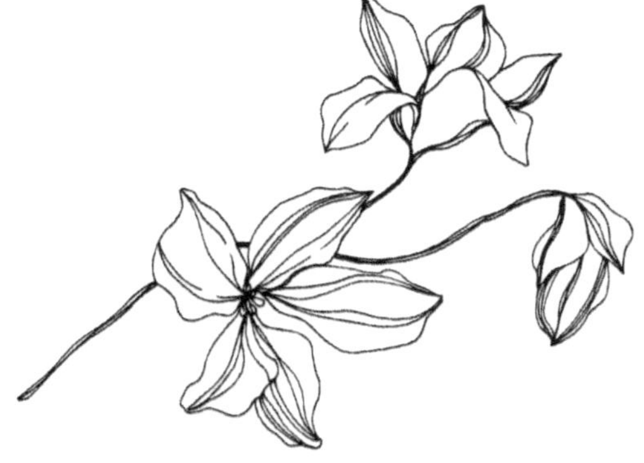

flower money

What he expects:
A girl should be…
competent enough to know how to straighten
her hair
presentable when around his friends
ready and willing to satisfy his needs
hygienically clean at all times
never expect him to buy her flowers even if
he does it once.

He communicates:
don't be so dramatic
chill out
don't be obsessive

And he gave me the flower money and said,
You can buy the flowers yourself.

Elle Daviau

Elle Daviau

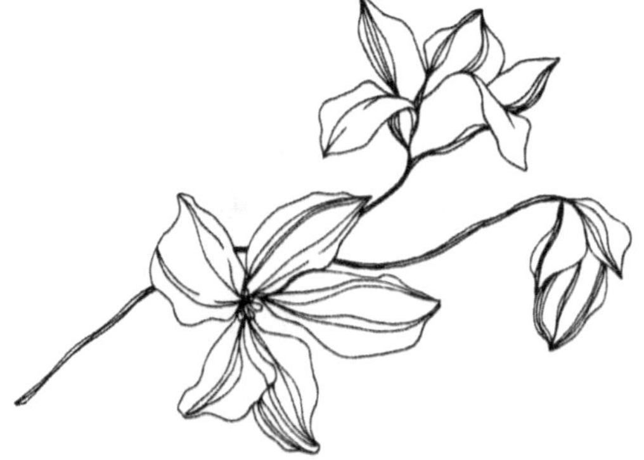

gunfighter

Laying in the bathtub
with my ears just beneath
the surface of the water.

The showerhead staring
at me becomes the feeling
of looking a gun down the barrel

or looking you
in the face.
They are the same: a risk

But everything's gone hazy blue
and I can no longer tell
your venomous snake bites from sweet kisses.

Elle Daviau

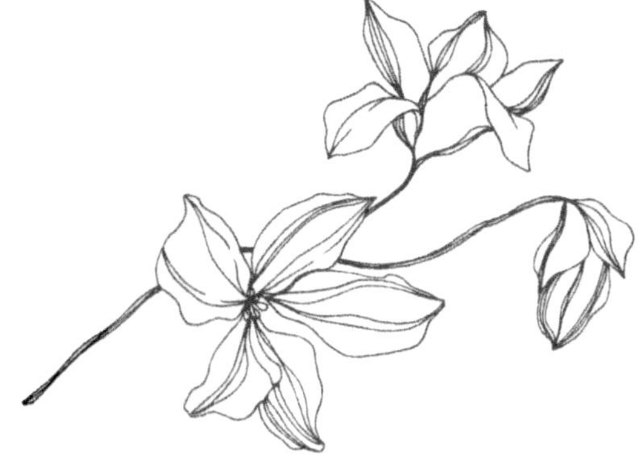

frôler la mort

Avec lui - PART 3

I dreamed of being with you
and what that does to me:

flowers fade

the leaves fall,

but in the midst of the seasons change,

we remember the love we shared.

The love I felt

and the vacancy

of where your heart left you.

Where your heart also left me.

Elle Daviau

Elle Daviau

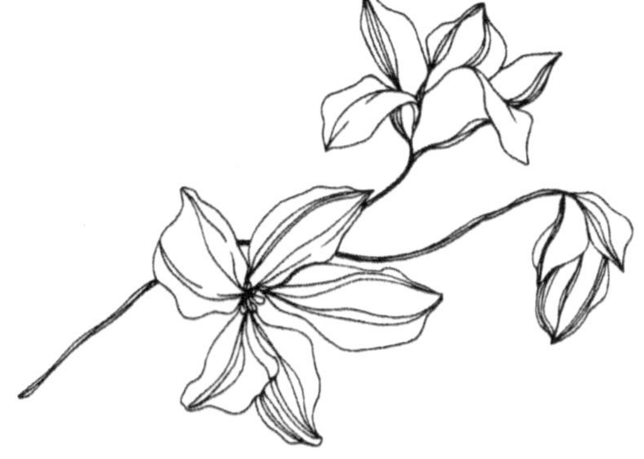

and these things will go by on your
walk through this forest

I've been murdered.

I know what it's like.

Not the kind of murder your soul loses

your body,

one of the mind.

But I lost my body

in a different way,

I gave myself away

and now it's still trapped with you.

Elle Daviau

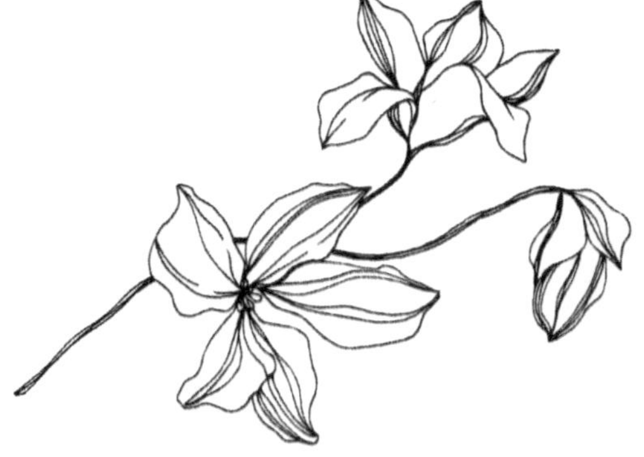

living on the moon

I spoke words to myself
In the sea of serenity,
It's strange, is it not?

What's that?
she answered.

The way people present themselves.
I leaned in for a kiss,
looking for love,
but all I got was a mess.

And I just continued
to sway
solemnly,
behind the moon.

Elle Daviau

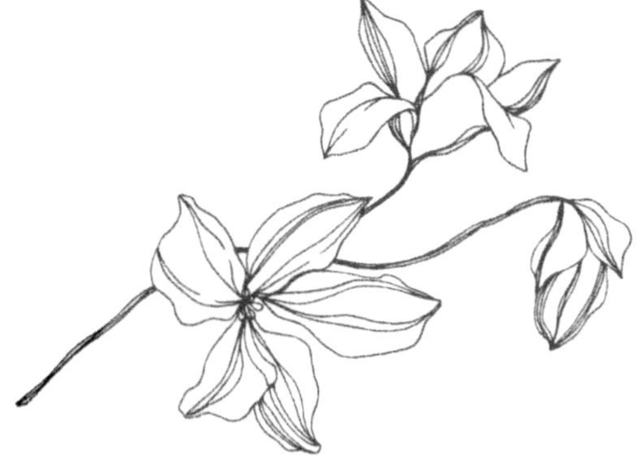

figura

I wondered how it must have looked out
there,
when February came and a sprinkle of snow
slowly coated the earth around us.
These mathematically perfect ice structures
took on the shape of me now — tattered and
broken.

I want to come back again, to the person I
was.
Time and space will no longer allow us to
reach for possibilities without the promise
of risk —
the risk worth taking for us.

Elle Daviau

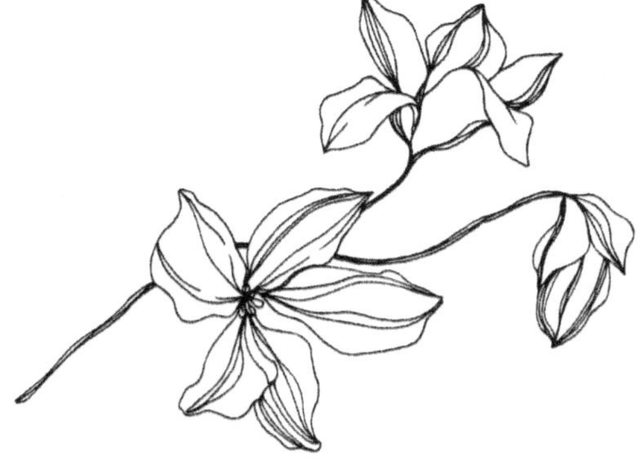

under the stormy, blue light tonight

To kiss is to take in such beauty, all at once, and
instill hope and passion back through me.

To touch is to know you through your skin—
know the curves of your body and the
roughness of your hands.

A love that is filled with scorching fire as
butterflies flutter deep down.

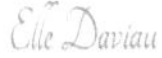

Elle Daviau

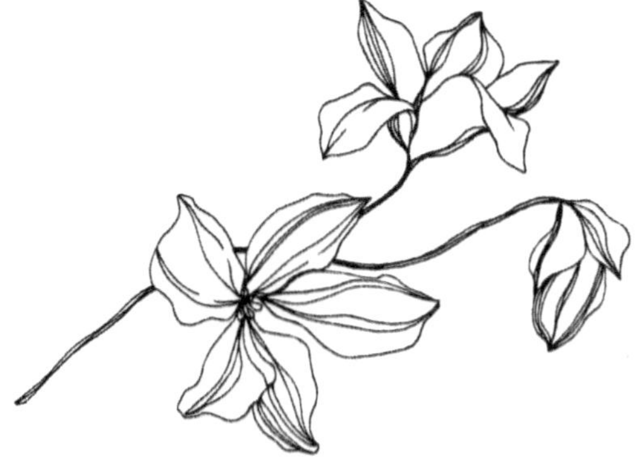

reclaim my reign

It hurts
to say your name,
I won't even whisper it to myself.

I want to,
so, I can cleanse my mind,
release my anger,
and regain my power.

My body stops me,
wells up cotton in my throat and
turns my lungs to glass.

Shallow breaths,
I return from my longing to hurt
then recover, for these are the pieces of my
mind
I cannot look back into.

These pieces
that would certainly end me
all together.

Elle Daviau

Elle Daviau

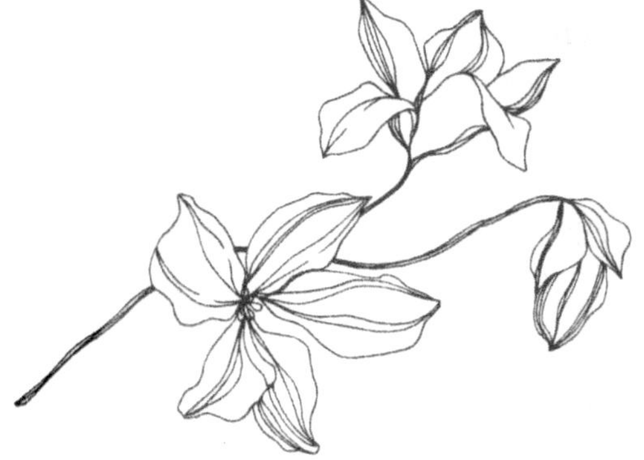

before

I miss the sunny days,
when light skipped
across the water
and shined through
the whispering trees.

Elle Daviau

Elle Daviau

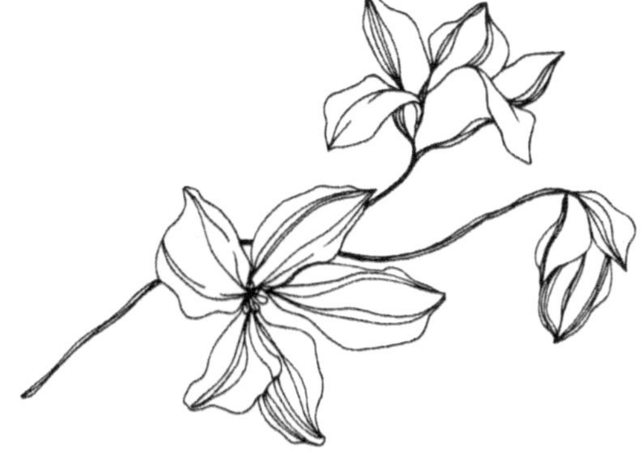

snakes under the stairwell

Our hearts work harder
when they know they're in love.
They want to stay,
they want to be happy.

>>> They don't understand
>>> that to love,
>>> leaves us vulnerable.
>>> It leaves us in need of *the one*.

But my heart doesn't know that my *one*
is seething
with viciousness after dark.

Elle Daviau

Elle Daviau

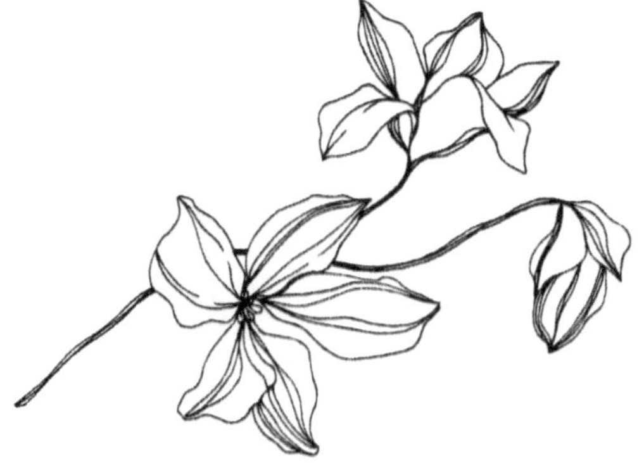

hummingbird feathers

Wrapped in his arms
With the blanket of the night sky covering his
psychopathy.
Covering all that he took away from me—

my purity.

Elle Daviau

Elle Daviau

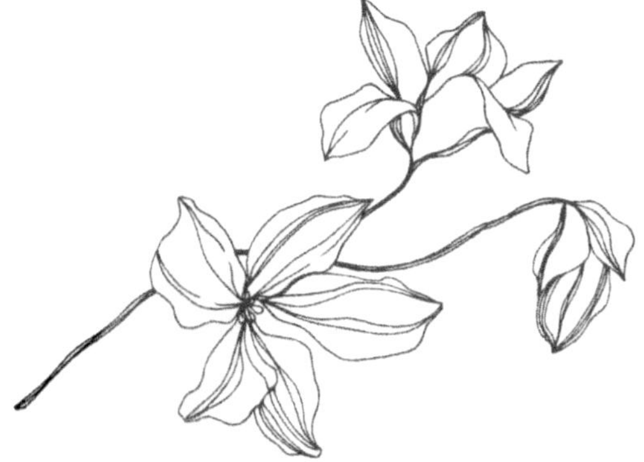

the blacksmith

the devil is real
he kissed me in my sleep last night
and did what he needed to get by unnoticed
in the light of day.

leaving the burden of his darkness with me
fusing my mind
into a warped image of himself.
my former self colored
him psychotic
after dark.

Elle Daviau

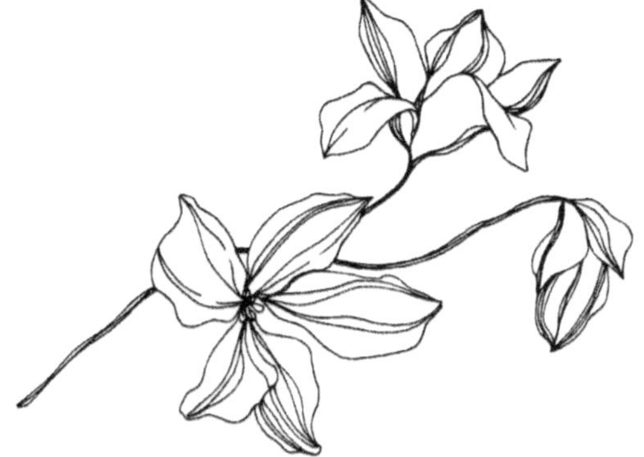

Lemon Thyme

Trichomes throw off sharp scents when the
wind comes through the
lemon thyme leaves on the terrace

The world seems never-ending when civil
dusk surrounds me
This darkness is different from him

When he was gone
My freedom was never fully given back
until my memories faded

He does not contain me anymore
Nor do I allow him to exist in my mind.

For the first time
I truly felt sovereignty.

Elle Daviau

Elle Daviau

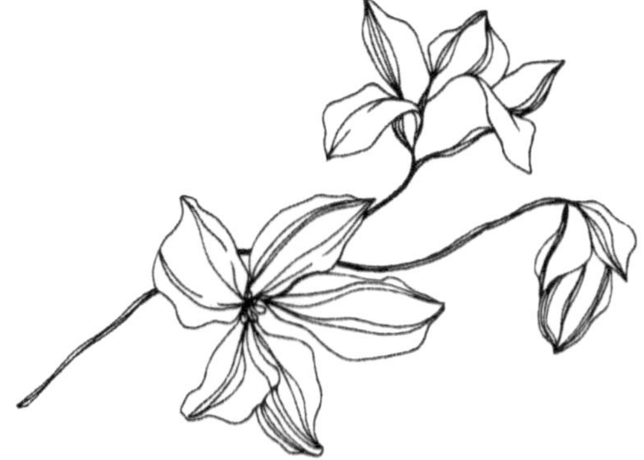

reincarnation under his light

Sunlight dripped
from the screened doorway to the kitchen.
Slowly,
then fast all together.
The windows drew me in,
speaking words of purity.

The chasteness that I so long for.

Elle Daviau

Elle Daviau

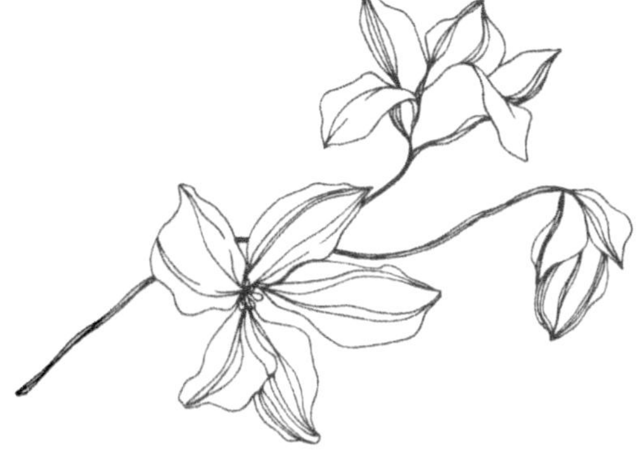

frilly violets over velvet leaves

Crystalline cell structure surrounds
my heart, like the skin of a flower petal.
I'm delicate to the touch.

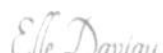

Elle Daviau

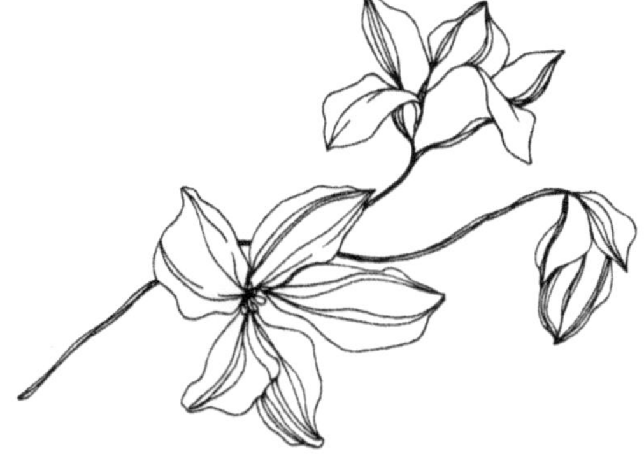

Milkweed

Your

      kisses

          are sweet

               and slow

          like honey runs through

               your veins.

You

      learned

          to lace your

               sharp words

with this after I discovered your

             truth,

   it brought me

      back to you.

          Back under

            your control.

Elle Daviau

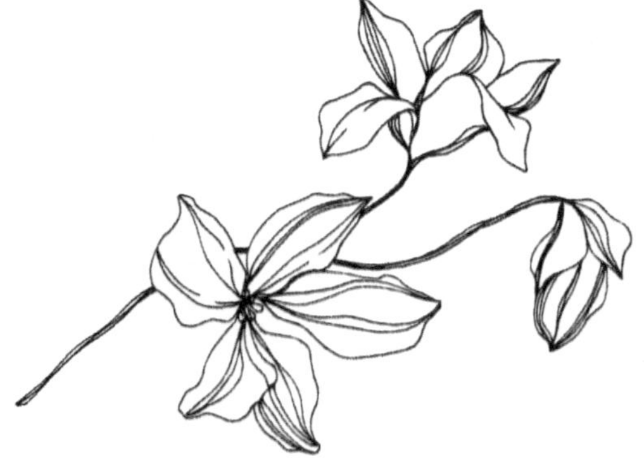

Exoskeletons

He was the point in my life at which all
roads met.

Unavoidable.

The tragedy to my myth in which I could not
forget.

Where I had to learn how to go on without
my former self.

Elle Daviau

Elle Daviau

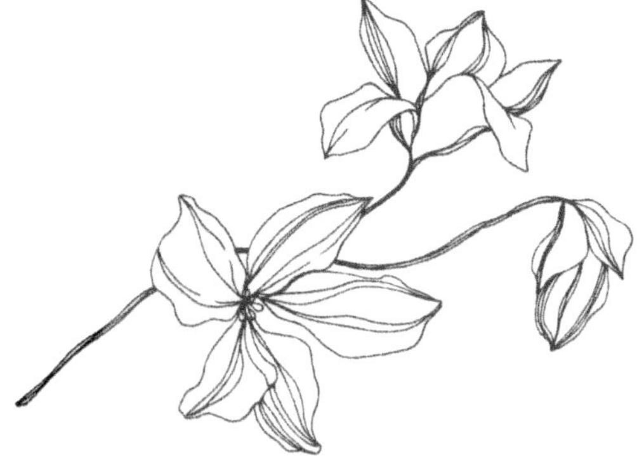

like strawberry skin

Violet clouds whisper
through the night sky.

Lavender blushes
through my veins.

Infatuated with wishful dreams,
I fall asleep.

Elle Daviau

Elle Daviau

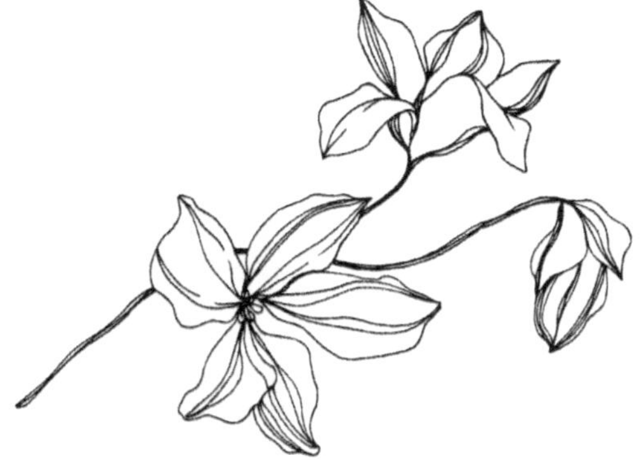

under this ice

I've been swimming
this ocean of thought
for a while now.
Soon I'll have forgotten
how to stay afloat with you,
and breathing the water
will become familiar to me.

Elle Daviau

Elle Daviau

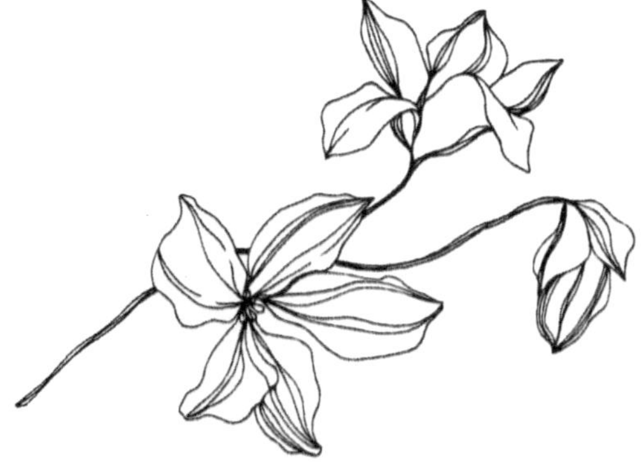

hermit crab shells

Dust connects
and I cannot see anymore,
I'll have to wait
for the break of light
shining between the tattered blinds
into this empty room
that you call home.

Elle Daviau

Elle Daviau

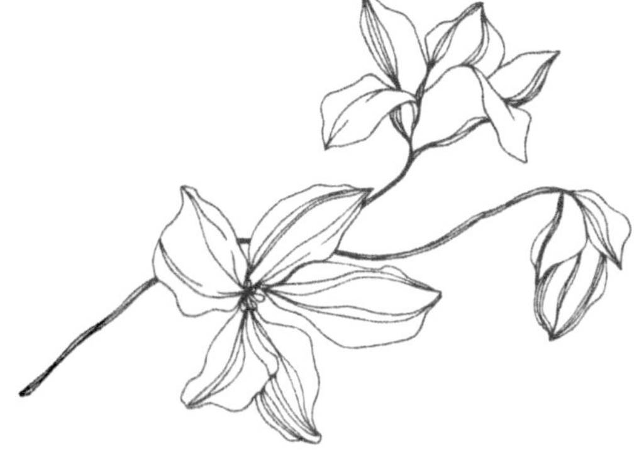

l'imperatrice

Summer rain on the rhubarb leaves.

Warm air holds me into my body.

Without it I would dissipate into nothing.

You, summer air, are the reason I persevere
for I cannot let them see my weakness—

The weakness he crafted into me,
chipping me away.
Before him, I was a godly stone sculpture made
with the finest hands—
they cared for me.
These breaks in me wreak havoc on my ability to
lead but these breaks, they must not be shown.

I continue to shine, stripping away the pain he
left inside of me.

And this summer air heals me a little more for
tomorrow's day.

Elle Daviau

Elle Daviau

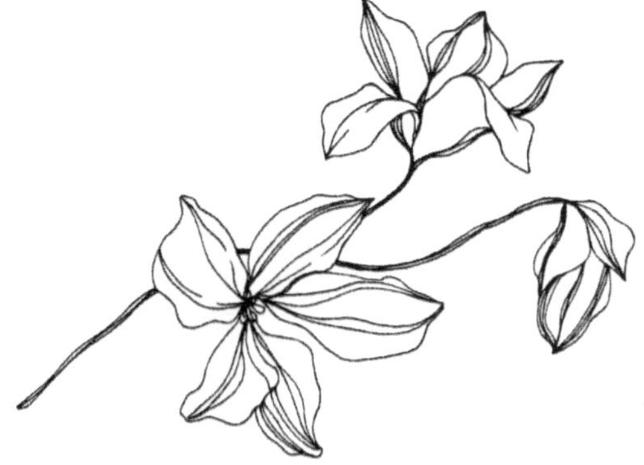

Heavy Waters

The ocean screams,
mist fills my eyes
The waves crawling past me—
they knock me down.
Drowning was all that I could do, my love.

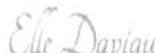

Elle Daviau

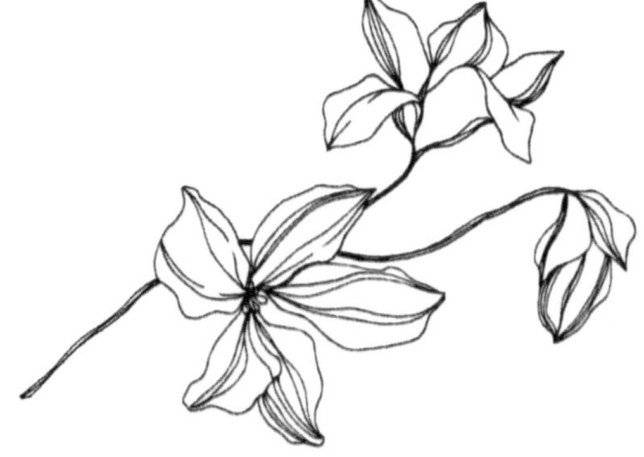

Black Death

I feel I love too much.
My heart has eaten my chest.
I am no longer free
of this eternal plague we call love.

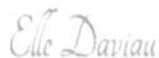
Elle Daviau

Elle Daviau

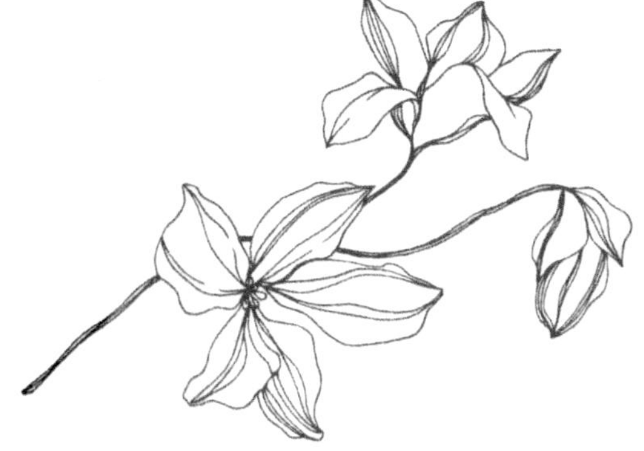

Absence

I love being adored.
But being adored in a vacuum,
there's not enough air for me to breathe,
to survive.

Elle Daviau

Elle Daviau

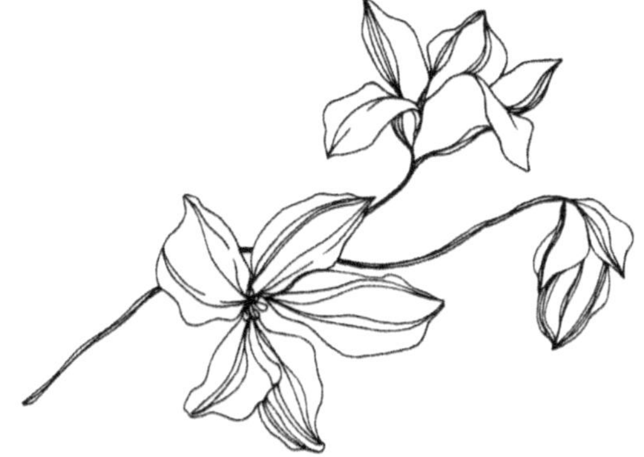

Morning Clove

Sparkling water guides my way down the road
and it makes me remember the ocean.
A dandelion blows in sideways across the grass.

Fresh sunlight guides my way.

I rip a blank piece out of the newspaper.

My Love,
please tend to my wounds.

I write in perfect pretty cursive.

I leave the note with an edge under the
planter by the door.

He'll see it someday.

Elle Daviau

Ocean Storms

Out on the dock the old fishermen sit
patiently.
The air was silent,
and crippling cold shadows bring me to my
knees upon the rocky shore.

The memories flicker in my mind like
they're on a carousel slide projector.

And everything was the same that summer,
the hot still air crawling over my skin

where his raven hair echoed darkness against
his alabaster skin.

I cannot do what I am not capable of.
For I was made with a different heart than
his.

Sown with a loose stitching
that de-threads a little bit more every time I
allow my heart
to love you.

Every time I allow these images
to glimmer though my head.

Elle Daviau

Elle Daviau

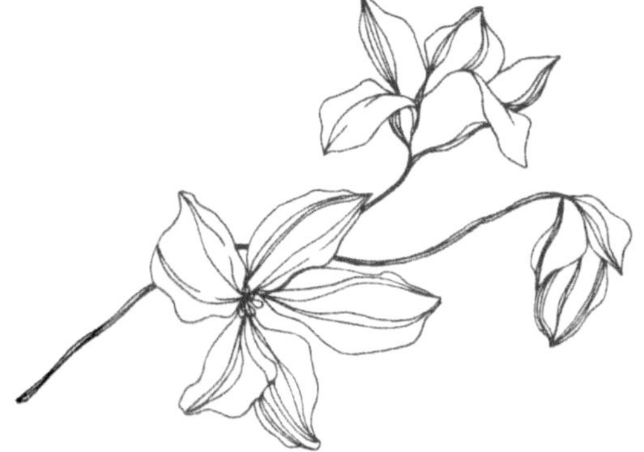

Callisto

Because one day
when the earth ceases to exist
all will be forgotten
and our existence will be but a distant memory
etching its way
into the history of everything.

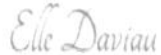

Elle Daviau

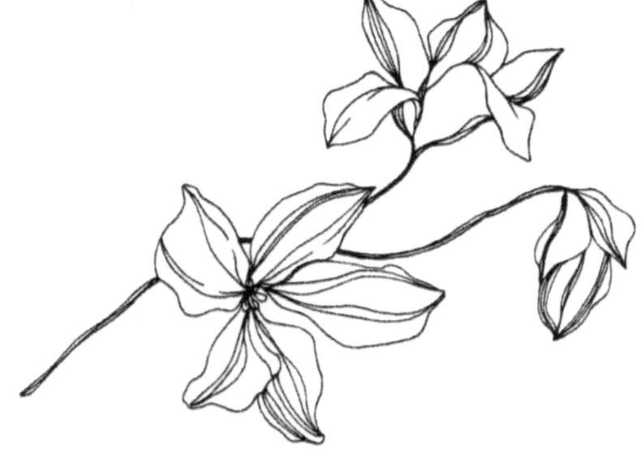

kelp tides

It's been a while since I felt
your wrath.
I'm still water,
waiting for the storm's anger
to strike again.

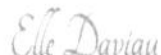

Elle Daviau

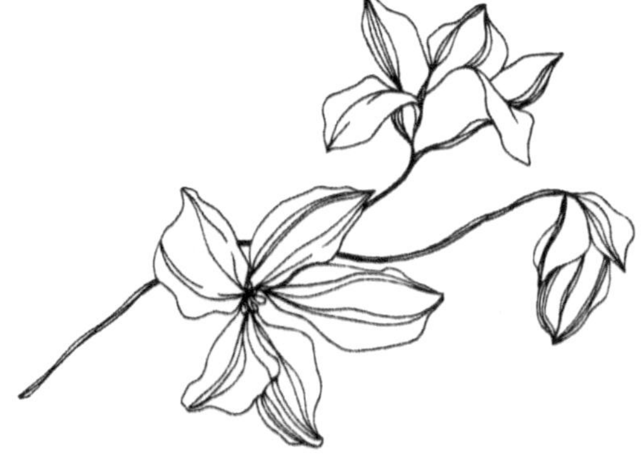

1989

What is the smell of spring?
A hint of cut grass,
fresh wind,
sunlight on my skin,
and I bury my face in the feathers of a duckling.

The birds are calling in the early morning,
looking to the sky, searching for the great
beyond.

Grass clippings staining the cold soles of my
feet.
Look for me, my sunrise,
and you'll find me where the flowers grow.

Elle Daviau

Elle Daviau

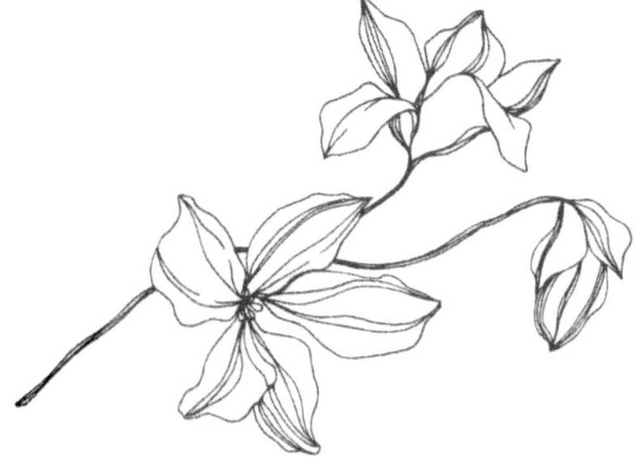

moonlight illusion

I remember that day,
when poetic sunshine splashed
across your softened face.
The day I saw you.

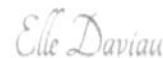

Elle Daviau

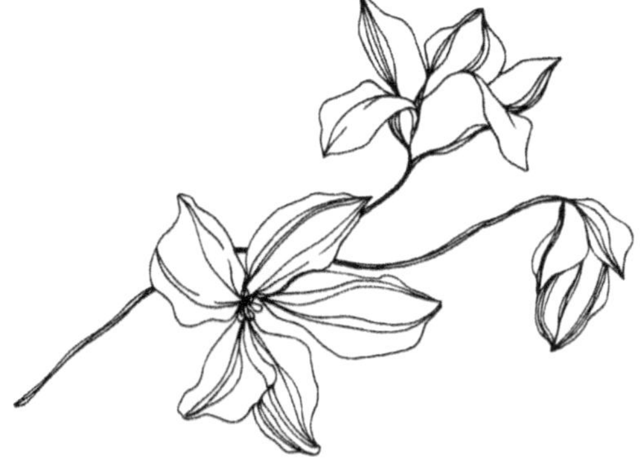

my mind is in a fizz, bubbling over
the rim of your lips

For a while, I'd left my body.
I went to a place far
from the grounds I lay on now.
The birds were calling from their perches
worried for what you might do
now that you've peeled
my conscience away from my body.

Elle Daviau

Elle Daviau

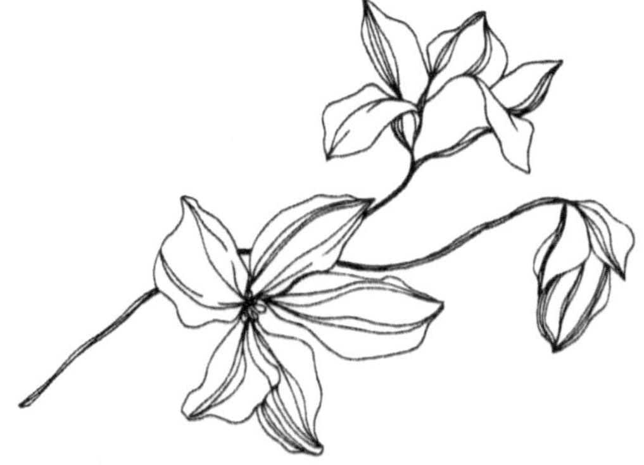

The Methane Sea

There was a distinct scent of raspberry when
it began to rain. Sudden and instant.
Soon the divots in the pavement were filled
with puddles.

I stand while the liquid methane
cleanses me,
breaking the barrier between myself
and the world,

running through the curves and creases
of my skin.
My reluctance fades.

I long for that gentle touch from another,
the one who can relax my mind.

Elle Daviau

Elle Daviau

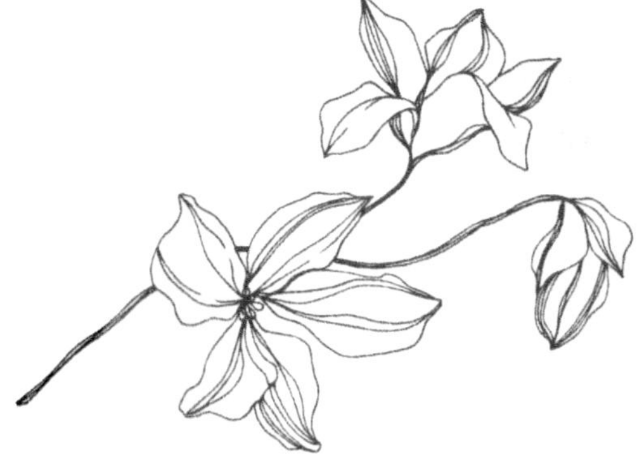

pierre de quartz

Many are blinded by love,
losing themselves as their own person starts
to fade away
and their partner becomes more clear.
It's the person that they see when they look
in the mirror,
but that'll never happen to me.
You took my sight away
when you had me, and now I'm left with the
symptoms
of your toxic grasp around my neck.
Broken, my love,
broken by you.

Elle Daviau

Elle Daviau

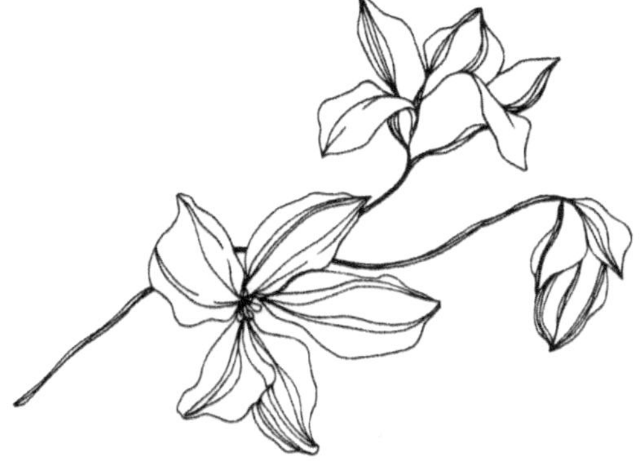

Obsidian

I desperately want to believe you,
but your eyes say differently.

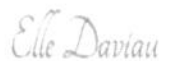

Elle Daviau

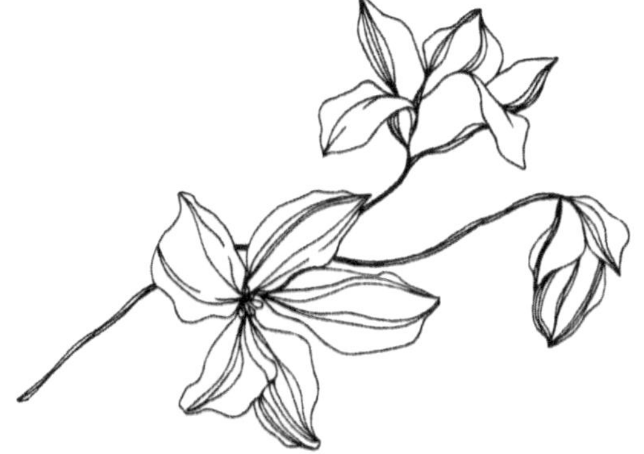

Shutter

Wishing I could cut off the pieces of me you
touched,
they've been long dead.
And I've become a forgotten garden in another
land,
my beauty distant in time
from the moment you closed the gate.

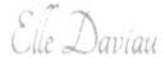

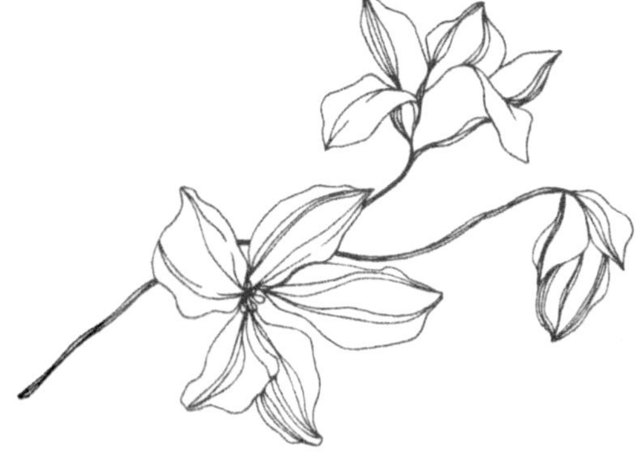

sickeningly sweet

A sweet smile
kissed my lips.

Like cherry candy,
my cheeks flush
under the palms of your hands.

Those touches that were cloying
from the pressure
of your lovely, dangerous mind.

Elle Daviau

Elle Daviau

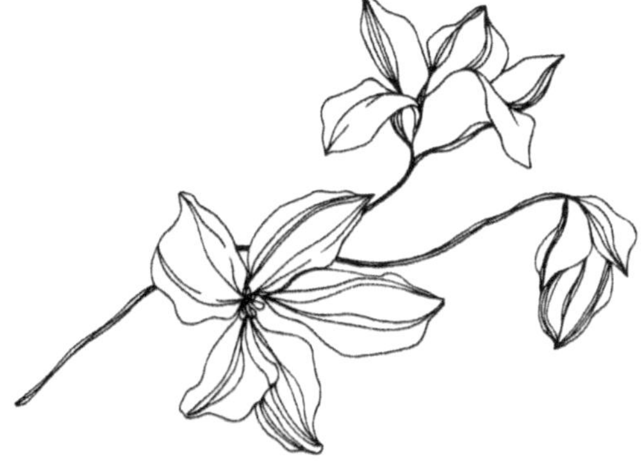

grey sky and mourning sun

Green light that passes
under the dappled clouds. I can no longer find
my strength when you relentlessly
take it away from me.

Elle Daviau

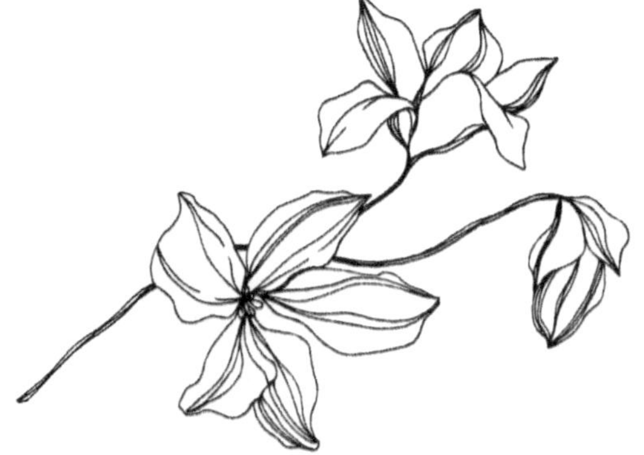

cottonwood trees

The cotton seed
floating on the wind
reluctant to touch the ground.

I'm your cotton seed,
everything I do
I cannot seem to come back home.

Softness that feels comforting.
Away, I see clearly.
I was hindered when I was with you.

I ameliorate as the pain subsides,
I am stronger
because I lost you.

Elle Daviau

Elle Daviau

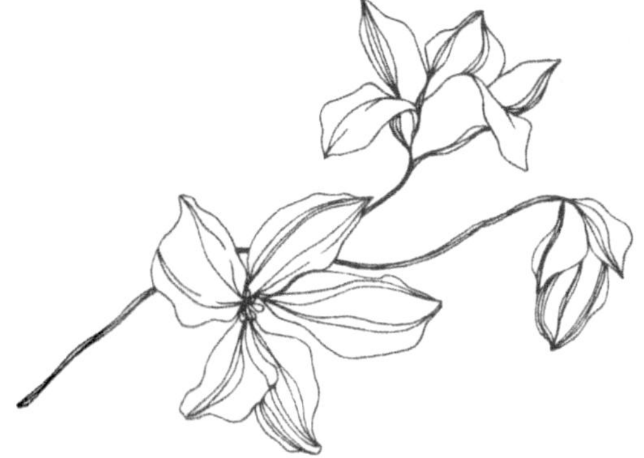

marshmallow leaves

Your skin that shines like it is coated in a
dusting of diamonds.
You had me at summer's end
where the air smells like lush growth,
clouds at peak capacity,
and strawberries over ripened.
I want to go back there.
I need the feeling of dampened grass
beneath me where you laid me down—
where I took the last breath of my life before
you.

Elle Daviau

Elle Daviau

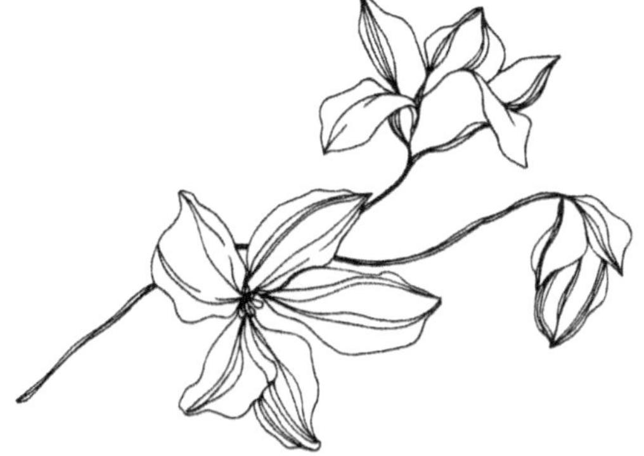

beneath the riverbed

Don't ever fight
for someone who doesn't
want you.

Elle Daviau

Elle Daviau

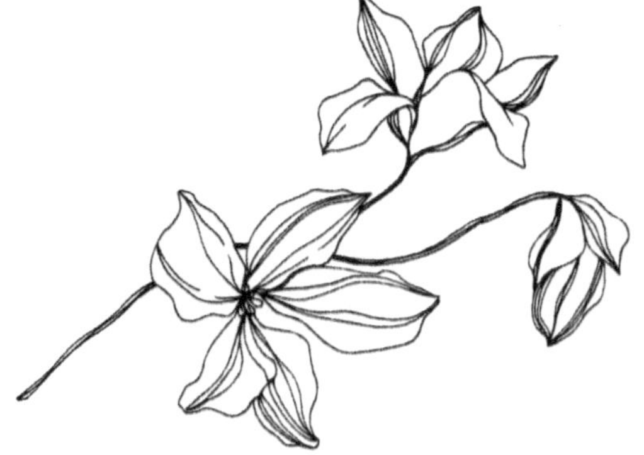

Through the Blueberry Fields

you step across the grass
your figure is diminished from the warping
through the windows
your shape
your build

I can no longer make the picture
I fear I will forever forget the way you were
constructed together

and I will forget the feeling
of being left
by a ghost

Elle Daviau

Elle Daviau

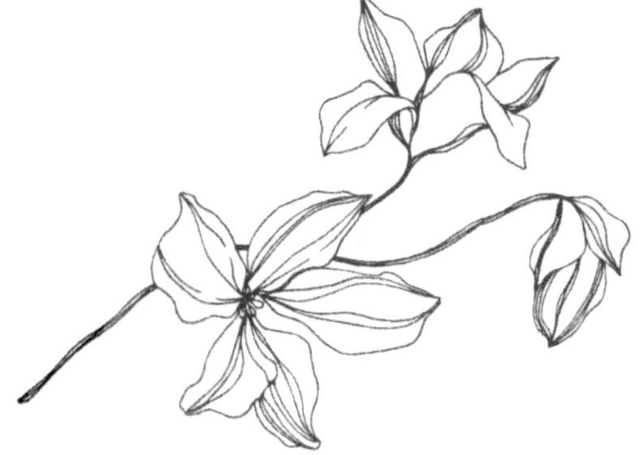

Persephone

Black birds in the trees
she pretended
to love me,
for I am an evil man
and that is why I must ruin her.
Her flowers must wilt,
the old oak trees must die,
and she must stay—
Stay here with me in the underworld
where she'll learn
to love me for the rest of her life.

Elle Daviau

Soleil de Minuit

She reminded them of the sun &
the scent of pachouli exuded from her skin.

But she had fallen sinful.
Just as where they found her in the sea of
serenity,
the dark parts in the surface of the moon
were the same parts of herself that she showed
to the world
because it was easier to deter from the outside &
prevent others from seeing who she really was.
This way, they couldn't take away the sunlight
that filled her body &
transfused her veins under the exterior of her
lunar armor.

Much to her dismay,
It could not protect her from him.

For she was not aware her darkness attracts
tortured souls,
simply looking for a light fix.

In the Pale Blue Grass

And when they get a glimpse of her sunlight,
the frenzy begins.

Like starved vampire bats to her fragile body,
even if it meant taking all she had and more
after that,

he'd leave her decaying and regretful,
without a way of recovery to repair the damage
he ensued.

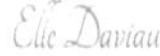

Elle Daviau

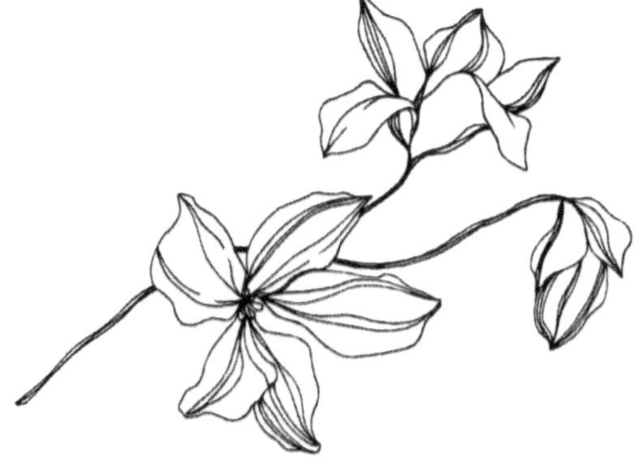

The Moon's Low Tide

Sometimes,
I do wish
I were a bird.

I could be an albatross soaring
the skies for most of my life,
through the strong winds
and deep water below
The water that gives me the answers
I'm in constant search for.
I believe they'd tell me to leave you.

But for now,
I'm here in human form,
looking for some way to abate my pain
unknowingly under the gaze
of my guilty
tormentor.

Elle Daviau

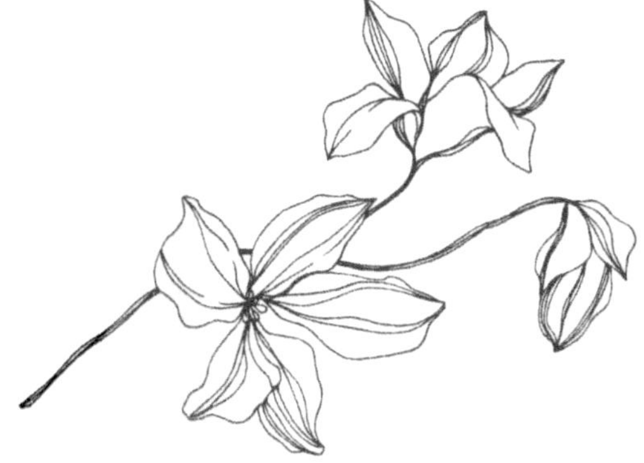

Lucifer

The devil is a quiet feeling
with a gentle touch.
He reaches
under your skin,
tells you soft lies,
and longs to pull
your heart out
with a sweet kiss.

Elle Daviau

Elle Daviau

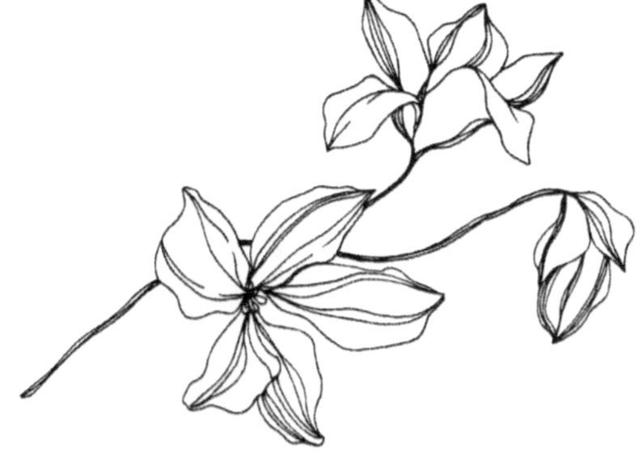

Black Moon Lilith

An impossible love,
between an alien and a human,
who is unhumanly herself.

I cannot maintain.

Elle Daviau

Elle Daviau

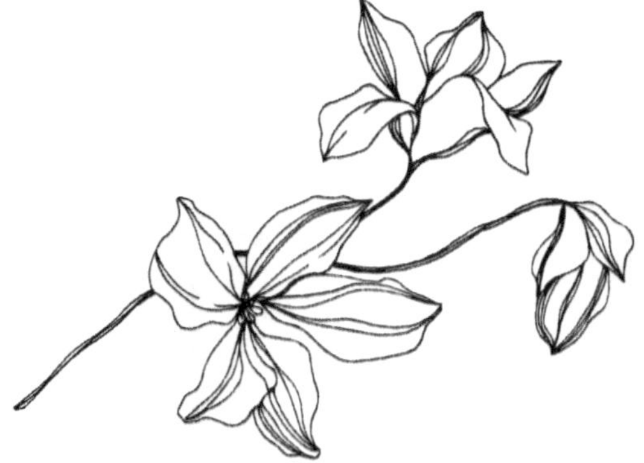

Angel

Like soft bodies
patiently wait.

Searching in the full moon's
dim light.

Elle Daviau

Elle Daviau

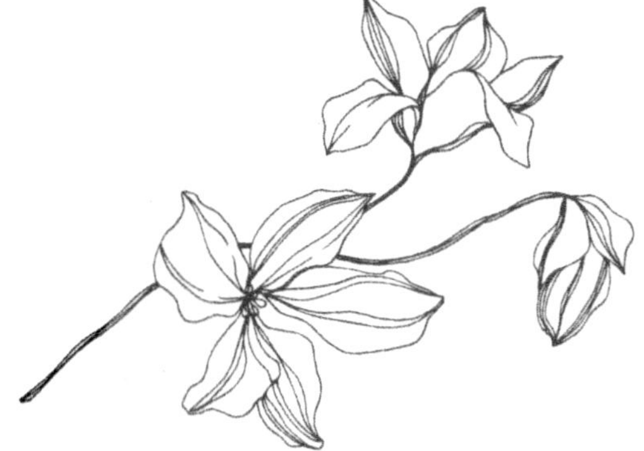

sugar words

He said the best things to me,
the kind of stuff that's only written in books.
And now I'm trying to be okay
with the idea
that none of it was true.

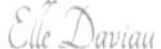

Elle Daviau

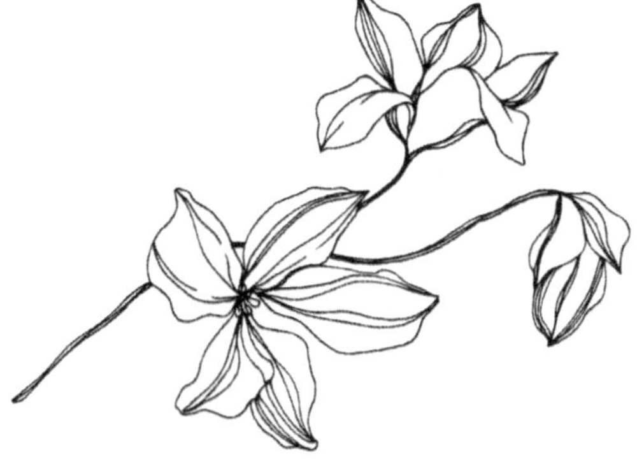

Chartreuse Sepals

Water drips down from the tall evergreen trees,
my face runs hot while my body stays cold
and unmoving.
This water — remnants of the summer storm
that painted the skies black
now sunlight sparkles off every surface.

The glowing life shows its gratitude
by reaching up for the heavens —
she answers, while I do not.

A breeze flows gently,
through the canopy of the forest
and further up, carries a golden eagle
high into our atmosphere.

Branches stretch in all directions,
blessing this forest with spurious rain
and washing away what he did to me.

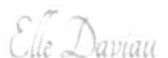

Elle Daviau

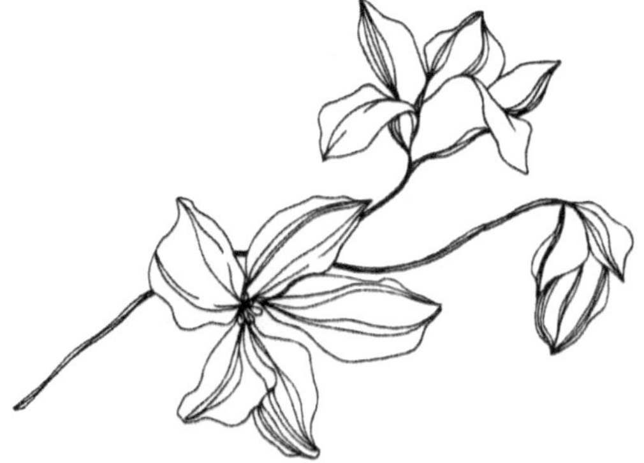

her

She's beautiful,
and also alienating.
an enigma that captures
all your attention.

She is ease, benevolence,
she's made of illusions and deception.

She has a fluidity
to her madness, it invites me in.
Much like Death
coming in on his boat to retrieve a soul,
yet he takes another,
for she is an unattainable beauty,
and you'd be a fool
to forget
she's dangerous.

Elle Daviau

My killer

I could only ever paint him
with closed eyes.
They were so dark,
filled with nothing of comfort.
To look into them
was to look into the dark abyss or to fall
into the universe for all of time.
No emotion, no conscience.

After a while I figured out that the person
he pretended to be,
really wasn't him at all.
I can't imagine the thoughts and terrors
of what goes on in his mind.
He speaks of death,
destruction of other people's lives,
and bestowing pity from everyone
as his only purpose.
There really wasn't any *him* to be seen.
He was nothing,
no one,

In the Pale Blue Grass

a horrific creation
that the world wanted me to see.

So, I painted this,
some sort of twisted beauty
of the darkest thing I've ever seen.

Elle Daviau

Elle Daviau

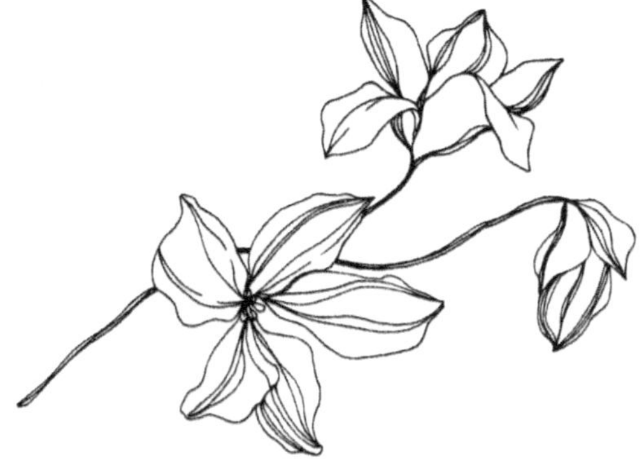

silver and white-furred rabbits

And it's killing me
on the inside.
Trapped
in your castle
made of lies.

I can only hide
behind the bathroom door
curled in the tub,
when your monster
comes out at night.

Elle Daviau

Elle Daviau

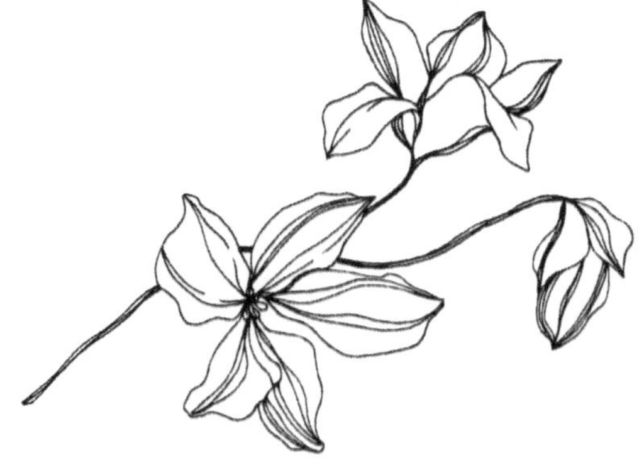

Collin

I love morning like how it is here today,
cool air deceptively hiding
from you the beauty of the day.
And the birds—
cooing doves and trilling hummingbirds.
Their simple needs for life
remind me that love and pain
are thought to be of one
and the same,
passing and persisting
in the ebb and flow of life.

Elle Daviau

Elle Daviau

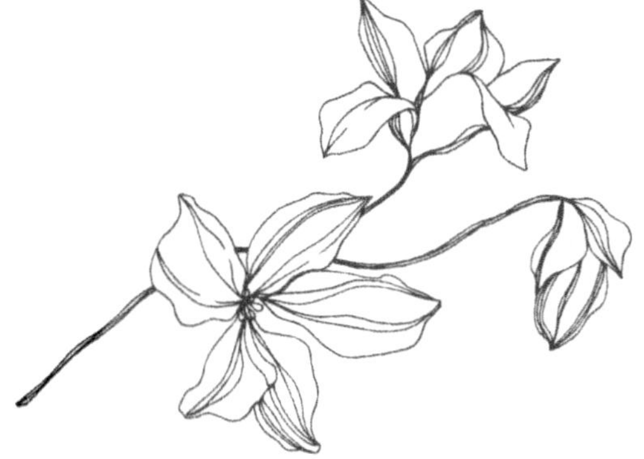

Gush of Unicorn Blood

even at night, clouds
refuse to turn as black as
the recessive sky.

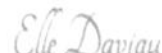

Elle Daviau

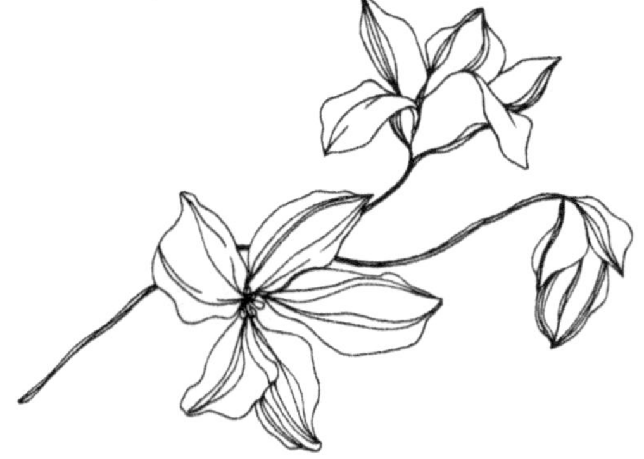

Mushroom Caps & Snail Shells

She imagines herself lost and hidden away
like raindrops falling to the earth,
unattainable and singular, yet plain in sight,
never to be found.
In a storm, they forget their way
when the wind sweeps
them aimlessly through the air.

Did you lose her when you laid
her down to sleep?
Was it a mistake of him to neglect her care?
She cannot fathom your actions
were as intended.

She can only believe that the love and
admiration were an illusion — a deception
for her to relearn to protect her incandescence.

Elle Daviau

Elle Daviau

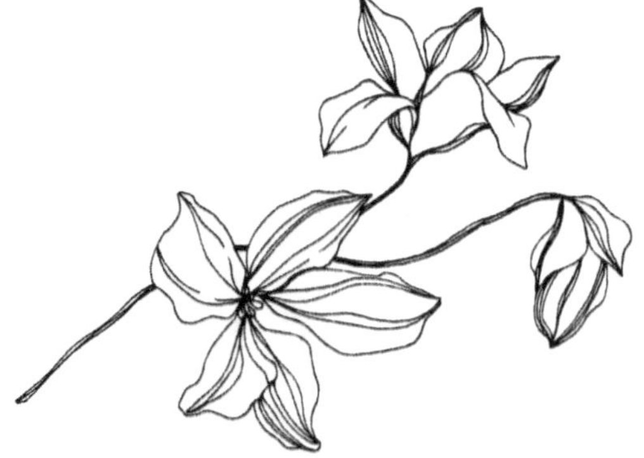

Calypso

The dark, cold wind drags along
with thick humidity in air
and the fog that fell upon the valley.
The valley with the enchanted waters
and green grasses that stretch over the pond.

And a girl, as beautiful as a fairy,
lays outstretched,
forlorn for the discord in her affairs.
She is enticing and captivating to them.
Yet, her heart belongs to another man.

Elle Daviau

Elle Daviau

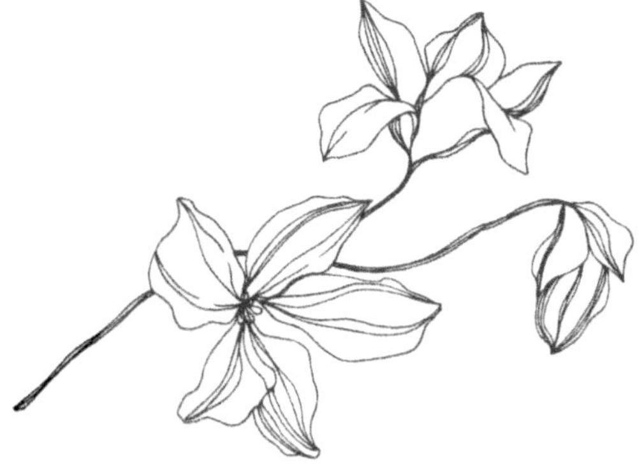

Oyster Shells

his heart can never break.
For what is lost,
can never
be broken.

Elle Daviau

Elle Daviau

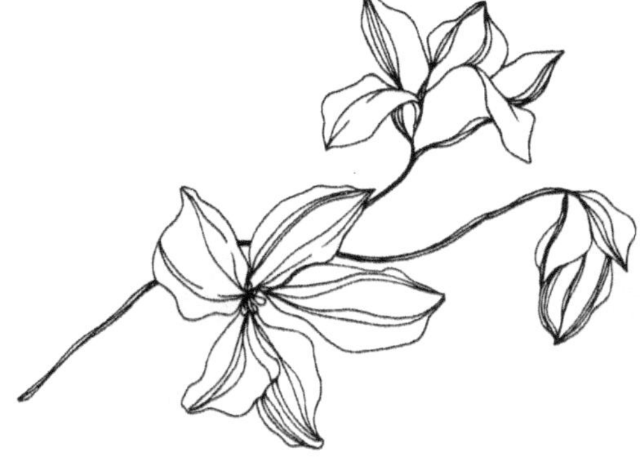

garter snakes

We are quite different.
You lie like it's the air you breathe,
you pretend you're someone you're not,
and you made me believe
that my life isn't worth living.

And *that,* is nothing like me.

Elle Daviau

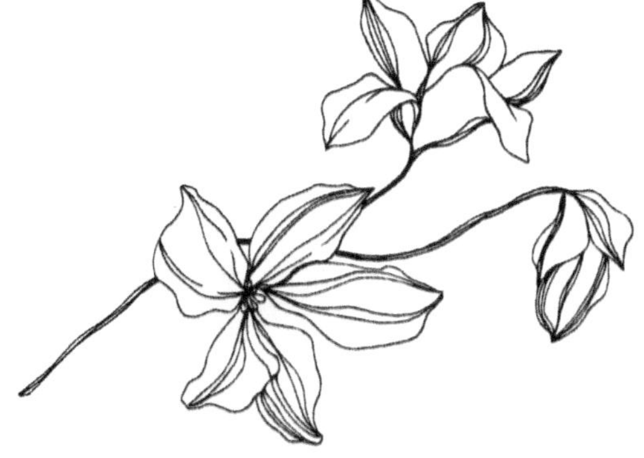

disintegration

There's truth
to the words you speak.
The ones dressed up
in an elaborate facade
designed as a joke.

I'm just teasing.

These words
they have meaning
they'll tear at me
little by little
until there's nothing left.

Elle Daviau

Elle Daviau

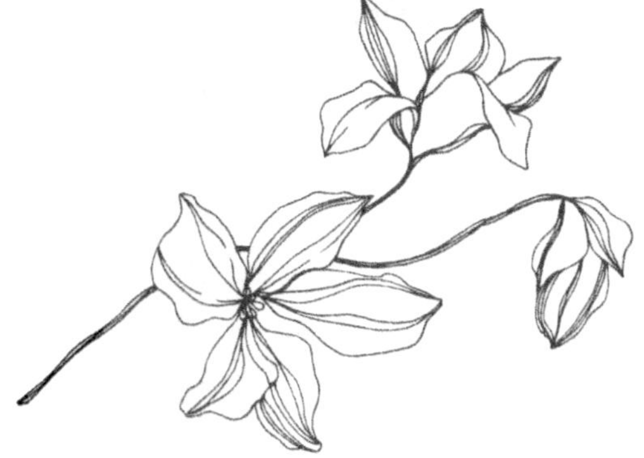

the lamb

Cool winter air fills my lungs
when I realize the mistake I'm making.
You, sacrificing me will not be my dilemma.

Elle Daviau

Elle Daviau

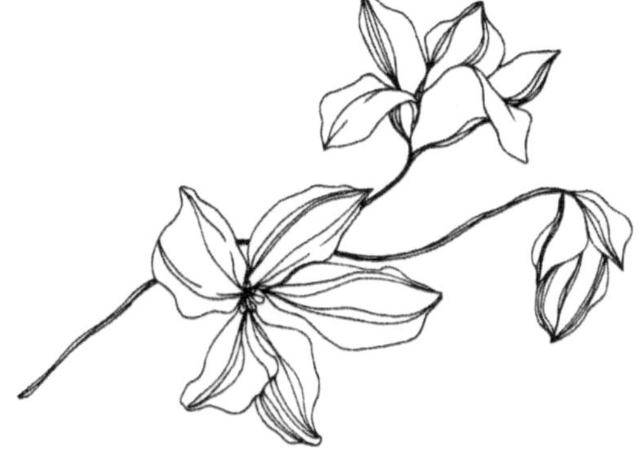

About Spencer,

The world felt different that day.
I knew
you had entered your eternal rest
you were never to be woken from.
A sleep so deep, not even true love's kiss
could bring you back.

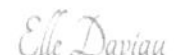

Elle Daviau

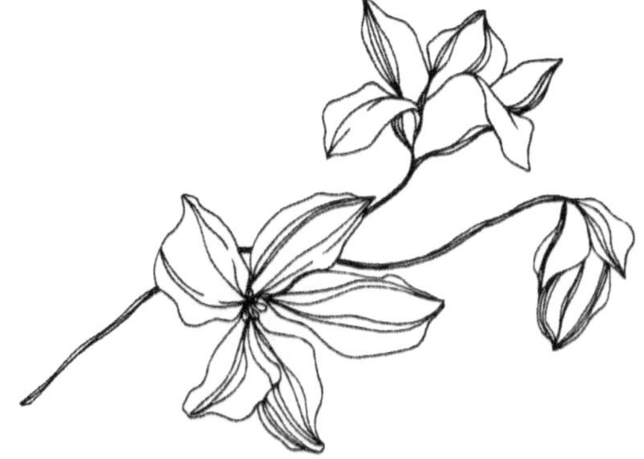

Under the Bamboo Leaves

Voices fade and I can only hear the grass
fluttering against the sky,
Like how the birds go silent after dusk.
Much love has washed away.

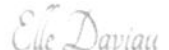

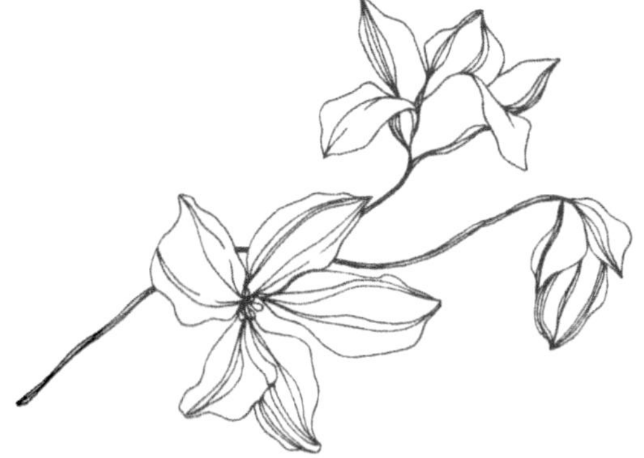

paper killers

I learned at some point that emotion is a gift,
if I'm blessed enough to have it,
then I owe the world to express it.
That's when I learned it was okay
to laugh out loud,
and love deeply,
and feel dark pain in times of sorrow.

Elle Daviau

Elle Daviau

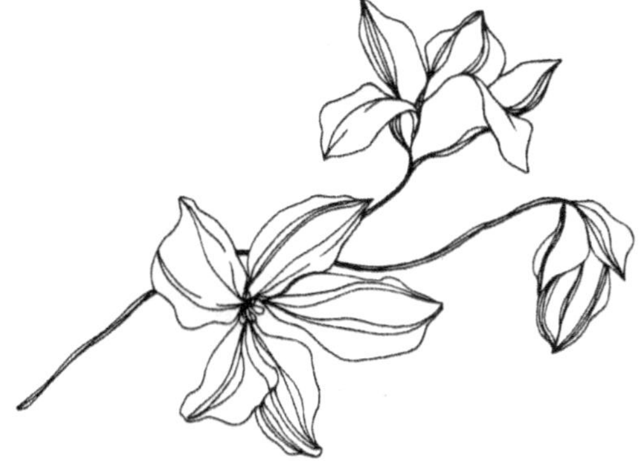

these cold hands can hold on

You know
that I have a fragile heart,
and this just hurt it too much.

Just a subtle look
That strikes the wrong chord
it could fracture my last vein.

The last
one you left
for the ultimate blow.

Elle Daviau

green leaves on lemon trees

I could be mistaken,
but this wind that is you rushing
through the leaves in the trees tonight
sounds a lot like the waves of the ocean
crashing against the shore
over and over again.

I could be misjudged,
for my eyes and my raspberry lips
seem to draw in
those who are unwanted,
unwaveringly broken,
looking for new life.
Pure life
to take over.

I could be misanthropic,
for our bodies touching
feels like space,
the kind that leaves me cold
and untrusting—unfeeling.

For your image of an angel withers
away in my mind.

<h1 style="text-align:center">In the Pale Blue Grass</h1>

I could be misguided,
looking for someone
to fill the darkness in me
to give me an influx of feeling
only in bursts,
just as the wind gusts into the trees,
then takes it all away again.
Someone
that's right next to me
but you were never there.

I could be laying here tonight
in your arms
seeing through you,
blinded by my own sickness.
Just as I am by yours.

Elle Daviau

somniferium opium

The hot summer rain took
my fear away,

pulling at the night sky
to cast shadows over the poppy fields.

The place where beauty
does not foreshadow malevolence.

I see that in you,
laying there,
reluctantly photosynthesizing
and decomposing.
That's what sadness will do to you.

Golden girl floating through the wind,
we fall back.

Beneath these poppies we call home,
there is a place
we do not belong.

In the Pale Blue Grass

The place where we intend
to stay.

Elle Daviau

Elle Daviau

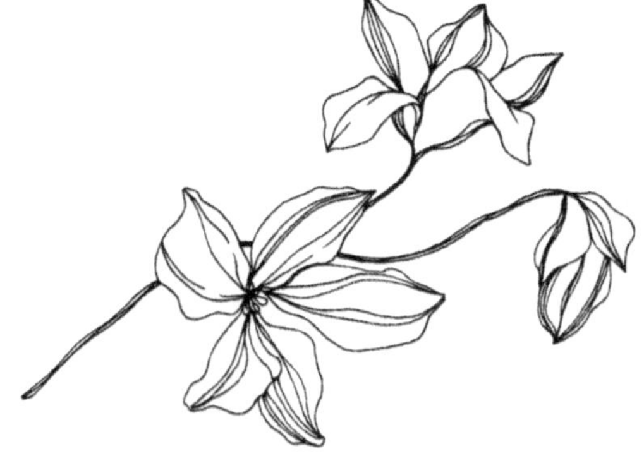

first snow fall

Sulfur street lamps
flicker on and off.
I sit,
and I wait.

My thoughts remind me,
He'll never love you more than your capacity
to love yourself.

Elle Daviau

Elle Daviau

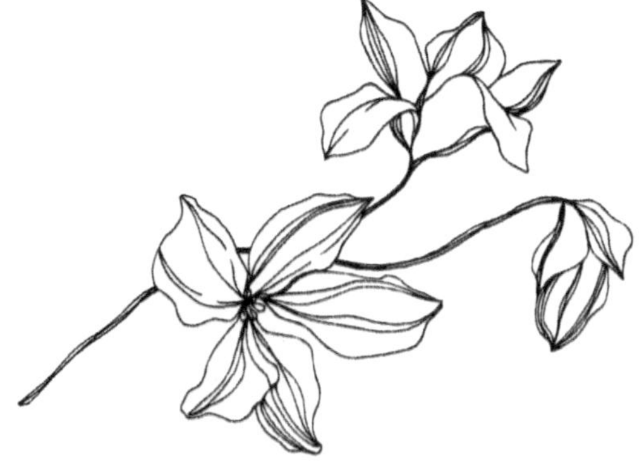

poppies enamoured in an alkaloid sea

I found you in the garden,

discourtesy,
he said,
was selected for you.
It takes evil to turn such beauty
into the destruction you have become.

The way skin grows,
and regrows
with a loving touch.

The presence of delicate petals
mistake you.

You cannot inure
yourself to the deadly toxin they leave
with you
when your penance
is time folded backwards.

Elle Daviau

Elle Daviau

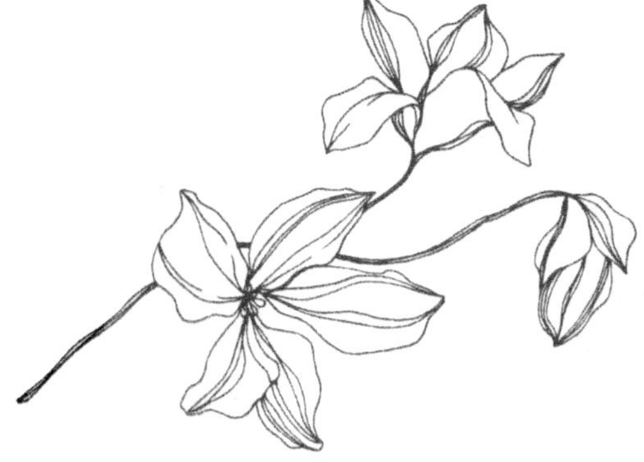

my love, let go

Address your soul,
let it find its place.
Here to stay,
take your rest,
and give yourself away.

Elle Daviau

Elle Daviau

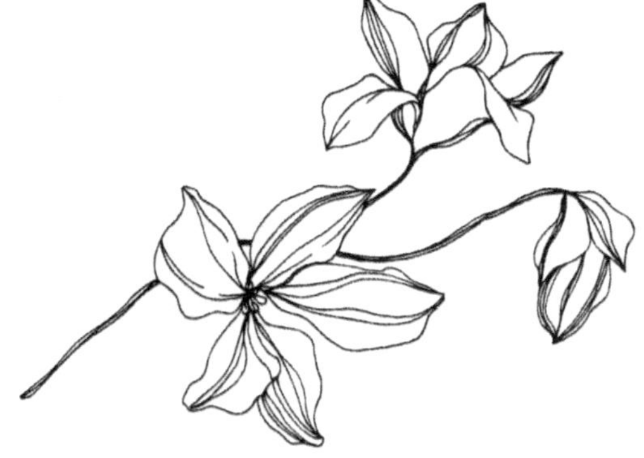

the duel

You know what it is to let yourself
be vulnerable?
It's holding your heart out in one hand
and a knife in the other.
And it's up to the other person
if they're going to take both,
or if they just take your heart
and hold it forever.

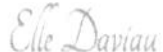

Elle Daviau

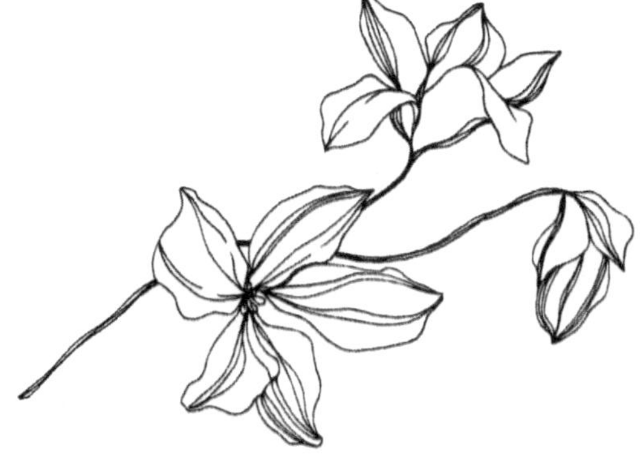

Beyond Angel Falls

But I love you,
she said.

Her words clear—
hankering for love
requited.

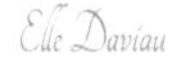

and then you
David - PART 1

In the fall.
when the day fades to night,
when the stars loom behind the cloud cover,
hanging
in the abyss of the pale, grey sky.
I wait patiently
for the wind to come.
It rolls in on gusts,
the way sea waves crash with tidal rock
up against the shore.
It screams through the branches
of the Douglas firs that surround me.
Those trees that look black
against this unlit canvas.
They move with the wind.
They collide with each other, angrily.
They look below
to me, resting at their roots.
This is no place for you, girl.

But I cannot help
my intent.
I cannot see the possibility
of a warm dawn—
not this night.
Not this life.
Not until then.

Elle Daviau

Elle Daviau

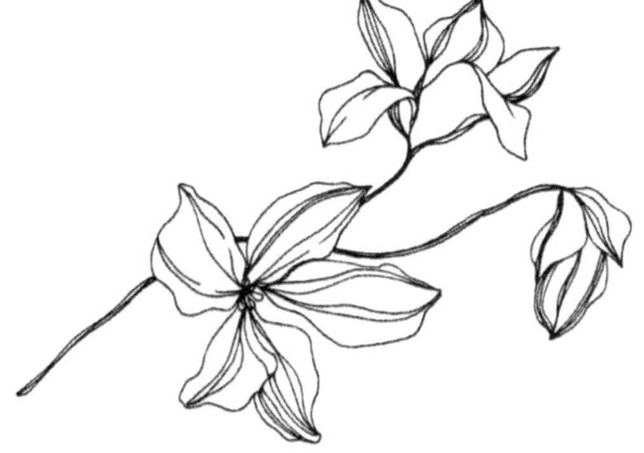

found

David - Part 2

Dandelions bribing me happiness
and the sunlight bringing in the rain.

The pink lining of strawberry sky
lies just beyond the silver clouds.

Up ahead is where I find you.

Elle Daviau

Elle Daviau

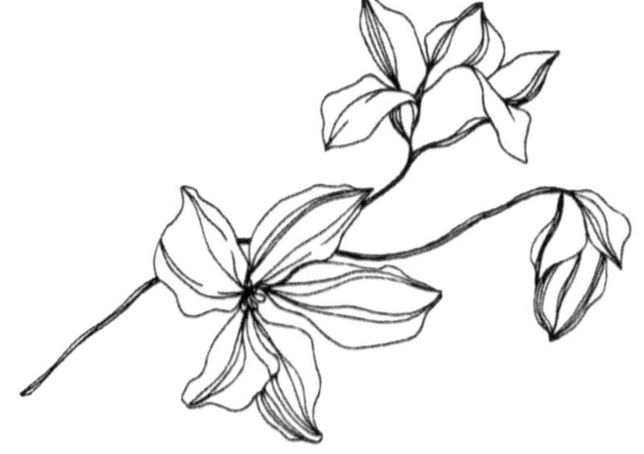

Genesis 1:3

David - PART 3

Follow the cycle of the sun and the stars
she said.

I'll find my way back.

You won't be lost forever.

Recovery will be my friend.

The time will come.

It's always darkest
just before the sun comes up.
I found my light.

He will be your light.

The sun stretching into my horizon.
In through me.

Be at rest.

He's here,
the sun and stars,
I was missing for a long time.

Ellie Daviau

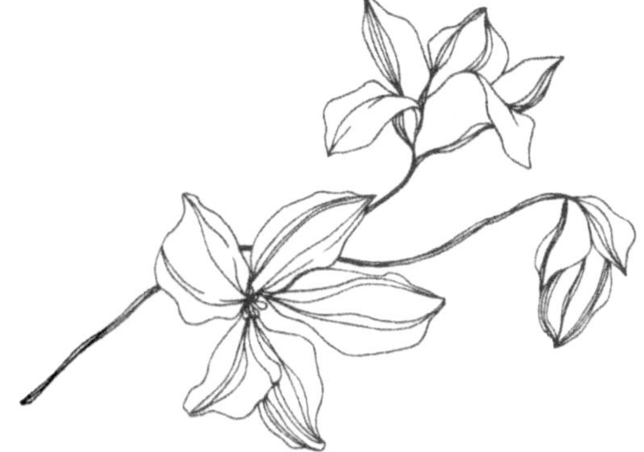

Pale Yellow-Eyed Grass

A love that's eternal,
persisting through winter storms
and the blaze of forest fires,

cherished,
especially on days,
where we rest so still
in the pale blue grass
on late afternoons.

Elle Daviau

Elle Daviau

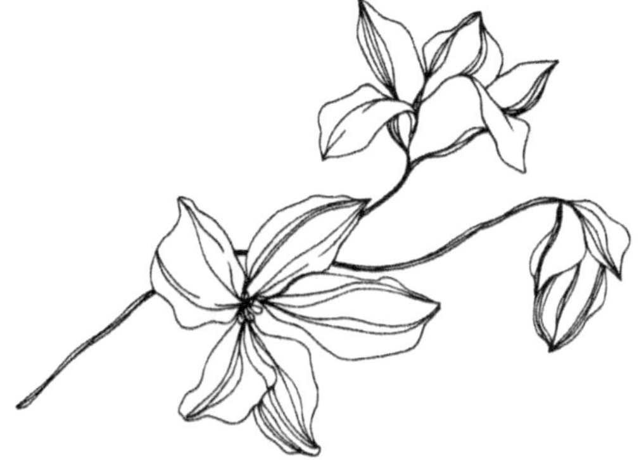

about the author

Elle Daviau attends college in the Pacific Northwest. She paints and writes poetry when she is not in a lecture or pondering life's answers in the starlit sky. *In the Pale Blue Grass* is her second poetry book.

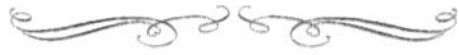

Other Books by Elle Daviau:
The Shores of Time

author website: http://www.elledaviau.com

Elle Daviau

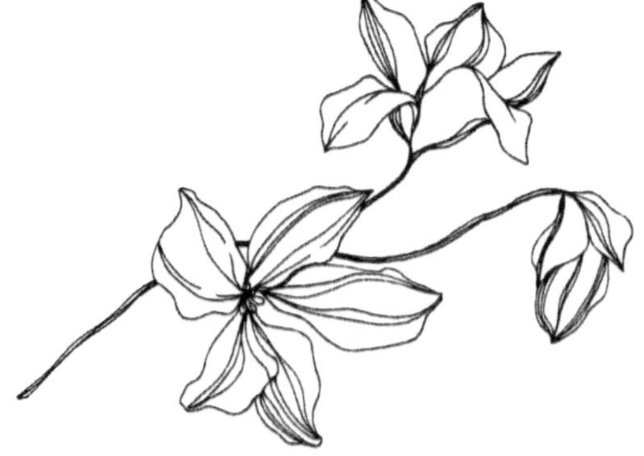

<u>*author note*</u>:

Thank you for reading my poetry. I know life is unbelievably short and your to-be-read book list is probably pretty long, so thank you for spending your time reading *In the Pale Blue Grass*.

If you do share your thoughts about this poetry book by leaving a review, please know how much I appreciate your time and effort for doing so. Thank you!

Elle Daviau

<u>Other Books by Elle Daviau:</u>
The Shores of Time

<u>*author website*</u>: http://www.elledaviau.com